Daily Thoughts

Volume I

90 Daily Readings for the Success-Minded Person

By

John Patrick Hickey

All Scripture text from the New American Standard Bible © 1960 unless otherwise noted.

The Message: The Bible in Contemporary Language © 2002 by Eugene H. Peterson

ISBN: 146117371X
ISBN-13: 9781461173717

To my loving wife Kate and my family.
Your encouragement, belief in me and
powerful love moves me forward.

To my friend Joshua Walker who first
encouraged me to put my thoughts in a book –

Thank you.

And to all my dear friends who have been a help
and inspiration to me. Thank you for your prayers and
support. You have been a great gift from God to me.

INTRODUCTION

"I consider my ability to arouse enthusiasm among men the greatest asset I possess. The way to develop the best that is in a man is by appreciation and encouragement."
— Charles Schwab

"But you shall remember the Lord your God, for it is He who is giving you power to make wealth that He may confirm His covenant which He swore to your fathers, as it is this day."
— Deuteronomy 8:18

I have always believed that each of us was created for a purpose. There was something that we are meant to do and no one else can do it for us. As I have been working with people for the past thirty years or so, helping them to find their purpose, I have discovered something important. Most people know they have something to do; they just have no idea how to find it.

This may sound like a simple issue, but believe me; the success of all of us depends on our knowing what we are to do. You will never arrive at your destiny if you do not know where you are going. The fact is that the majority of people alive today will one day die and never fulfill their purpose or realize their dreams. That is tragic.

Here is the good news, there are many who I call **Success-Minded People** who have that desire to find and fulfill their purpose. They know that the dream that God has

5

placed in them is in fact that very purpose they are to fulfill. For some it is to build a successful business or to go into politics, the arts, education or medicine. Still others are called to the ministry to fill a pulpit, found a church, do a non-profit work, evangelize or go into missions. You see, there is no end to our callings because there is no end to our God.

For far too long Christian people have seen their destiny or calling as only involving the church. They have had the desire and burning passion to go into business or some other "secular" endeavor but deny themselves because it was not spiritual enough. Businessman, W. Clement Stone said, *"When you discover your mission, you will feel its demand. It will fill you with enthusiasm and a burning desire to get to work on it."* But for many Christian people this has not been true. They settle for less in life because of some misguided idea that it honors God. This too is tragic.

God is not honored by mediocrity. Scripture tells us to do all to the glory of God. That means our best and for us to strive to be excellent in all we do. We are a **Success-Minded People** who know that we have much to give. Christian author and businessman, Zig Ziglar said it this way, *"You already have every characteristic necessary for success if you recognize, claim, develop and use them."* God has created you for greatness, to change the world. He is never lacking.

One of my callings is to encourage others to be the best they can be. My heart's desire is to see as many people succeed in life as I can. I live in the same world you do. I see all the negative and hateful things going on, the economy being destroyed, morals fading away from the public arena, our schools teaching nonsense and crime rising faster than we can keep up. However, I also see that there are good people in this world. I see people helping others in times of tragedy. I see a rise in those who would stand for what is right, just and righteous – Success-Minded People who believe in the principles of success and will add value to the world in which they live. In short, I am a hopeful man who believes that we, those who are **Success-Minded**, can change the world and make it better.

The time has come for us to seek change, not in the world around us, but in ourselves. We must first become who we are called to be, and then we will see that change affect others. Author of <u>The Pursuit of Excellence</u>, Tom Peters said, *"Winners must learn to relish change with the same enthusiasm and energy that we have resisted it in the past."* God created you to win. You are not becoming something you are not; you are becoming who you really are.

"Deal honestly and objectively with yourself;" wrote Brian Tracy, *"intellectual honesty and personal courage are the hall marks of great character."* **Success-Minded People** are people of character. They work at being the best they can be as a person. They have high standards for themselves and are constant learners. Personal development is a high priority for them and they will do what they must to grow as a person and in business.

The following 90 daily thoughts were written with this **Success-Minded Person** in mind. They are meant to encourage and to help you grow a little every day. Some of these lessons will hit home and cause you to make the changes needed to succeed; others will be more of a reinforcement of what you are now doing. In the end, they are geared to bring about change. Jim Rohn said, *"We generally change ourselves for one of two reasons; inspiration or desperation."* I believe either one will do if it brings the changes we need.

I want you to know something: I believe in you. How can I say that when I have never met you? Easy, I believe in the great God-given potential of all people. Yes, I am the first to tell you that some people will never reach their potential because they will never try. There are those who are lazy and what Scripture calls sluggards. However, I am almost certain they are not the ones reading this book. The person who reads this or any personal development book is a **Success-Minded Person** and has the potential to win in life.

I know you have a dream that is burning inside of you. Some of you may have started on the road to success to make that dream real. Others are just waking up to the possibility that you can really do this after all. *You can do it!* Do you hear me? You can do it, I know you can. Please allow me to be your cheering section. If you need to know that just one person does not think you are crazy and believes you can achieve your dream, then it is me.

I am so excited for you and this journey you are on. To think you can be that which you have always wanted to be. Time to get rid of the limitations, the excuses and the fear. Launch out into those uncharted waters and set sail for your own success. Believe in yourself and in the possibilities that you face. Nothing is impossible for those who believe!

"If you have zest and enthusiasm, you attract zest and enthusiasm. Life does give back in kind."   – Dr. Norman Vincent Peale

WHAT IS A SUCCESS-MINDED PERSON?

"There are people who make things happen, there are people who watch things happen, and there are people who wonder what happened. To be successful, you need to be a person who makes things happen."   – Jim Lovell

There is a difference between a successful person and a **Success-Minded Person**. While many of us achieve success in several areas of life, we have not finished the race. To me, we hit full success at the end of life. If we have fulfilled our purpose, achieved our dreams, made the world better by our being here and are loved by others, we have succeeded. Until that moment, however, there is always more to achieve, more to give and more to love.

Success-Minded People are those who have decided to take control of their life and to give their all to the fulfillment of their dreams. They are the people who are always improving, learning and serving. **Success-Minded People** know that even when a goal is reached, it is not the end. As long as God gives them breath, they have something more to do.

Success-Minded People know that true success in life is not based on money, power or fame. They understand that many of the most successful people in the world never make it to the pages of history books; some have little in the way of possessions; and are servants not masters. What they do possess is the satisfaction of knowing that they have fulfilled their purpose and have given more than they have received in life.

Success-Minded People also know that success does have its rewards. For some they are able to use their talents and skills to achieve great wealth, become a leader and change the world. It all lies in the dreams they hold and their purpose for being. The rewards are never the goal; they are the results of greater goals.

Success-Minded People understand that there are principles to success. There are natural laws that must be followed if one is to be truly successful. They understand that they must pursue wisdom and integrity at all times. They know that there are basic fundamentals to success that cannot be avoided or by-passed. They are *Honorable, Faithful, Servants, Friends, Mannerly, Caring, Responsible, Positive, Frugal, Courageous, Healthy, and Spiritually Committed* (Yes you have heard this list before. It is based on the Boy Scout Law).

Success-Minded People have vision and are determined to achieve their dreams. They are willing to pay the price of hard work and sacrifice to become the person they need to be in order to fulfill their dreams. Their goals are clear and well defined; they know where they are going and have a plan to get there.

Success-Minded People maintain a positive and cheerful attitude. They believe the best in people and in life. They know that every problem has a solution and whatever they face can make them better in the end. They possess the courage to reach beyond their abilities and to become better, stronger and more skilled. They are not slaves to doubt or negative thinking and fear.

Success-Minded People seek to serve others. They look for opportunities to be helpful and add value to everyone.

They are quick to encourage others to succeed and to give advice and direction when needed. They are givers and are willing to do what they can to help those in need by giving of their time, talent or possessions. They use wisdom in giving, always doing what is best for others in the end.

Success-Minded People are confident and believe in their dreams and the ability to achieve them. They know that God has given them all the talent and ability they need to fulfill their purpose. His call to them was with full intention to see it accomplished. They trust God for the power, wisdom and knowledge to be the very best they can be, and use that to bring glory to God's Name.

Success-Minded People know that they have much to learn and are constant students. They know that life is one long classroom; and they have something to learn from every experience they have, every person they meet and everything they read, listen to or touch. They take time for personal development and are willing to invest their time and money to become the best at what they do.

Success-Minded People are you and me. If you are reading this, it tells me you want more in life. You have a dream that is burning in your heart and you are doing your best to achieve it.

Success-Minded People know we are not alone, that others are on this journey and we can all help each other to succeed. Your success is as important to my success as mine is to yours. Together we can do this and make the world a better place.

"Success is a journey, not a destination. The doing is often more important than the outcome." — Arthur Ashe

Daily Thoughts: #1

STARTING OFF RIGHT

"Every time you smile at someone, it is an action of love, a gift to that person, a beautiful thing."

— Mother Teresa

Success-Minded People know that to achieve you must start off on the right foot. The best way to start is by giving. There is nothing you will do that is more important than adding value to the lives of others. Adding value helps everyone you come in contact with, and it will build you up both personally and spiritually. **Success-Minded People** know they are here on this planet to contribute, not to take from all around them.

The great coach John Wooden said, *"It is not a perfect day unless you have done something for someone who can never pay you back."* So what do you have of such great value that no one can pay you back? That would be a positive and friendly attitude. **Success-Minded People** know that a pleasant smile and hello, an act of kindness or maybe keeping quiet rather than speaking your mind are all part of a right attitude. A strong positive attitude on your part can make the difference between someone having a terrible day or having a wonderful day.

Success-Minded People know they must be pleasant to all with whom they come in contact. That, by the way, includes your family and co-workers. You work at building the reputation of being a kind and giving person. You will be surprised on how many doors this will open for you, as well as help you be healthier and happier. Studies have shown that people who have a positive attitude and are pleasant to others are sick much less than those who face each day with dread and anger.

There is a great old saying that I believe makes the importance of a positive attitude clear: *"All things being equal, the likable person wins. But all things not being equal, the likable person still wins."* **Success-Minded People** know that people cannot help but want to be around a positive, likable person. Likability will open more doors for you than skill, education or experience all together could.

"A cheerful heart brings a smile to your face; a sad heart makes it hard to get through the day."

– Proverbs 15:13 (Message)

❖ ❖ ❖

Daily Thoughts: #2

MORE THAN OKAY

"Refuse to be average. Let your heart soar as high as it will."   — A.W. Tozer

In a children's book I wrote back in 2002 called, **A Storyteller's Book of Tales**, there is a story called *Charlie Was Just Okay*. It is about a boy who wanted to be something but he was just okay. He wasn't a bad kid but wasn't perfect either. He wasn't tall, but he wasn't short, he wasn't big but he wasn't small, he was just okay. After fancying himself an explorer, rock star or a superhero he came to understand from a friend that *"being Charlie"* was very special all in itself.

Have you wanted to be something you are not? Have you dreamed that things could be different if you were smarter, richer, wiser or better looking? **Success-Minded People** have all had moments of wanting to be special. A desire to be excellent and stand out from the crowd is an attribute of **Success-Minded Person**. Another thing that makes us **Success-Minded** is that we realize that we are indeed special and created to be who we are for a reason.

God never created you to be average or to just get by. He created you for a purpose, a very important purpose. You play an important role in God's great plan for this world. You cannot fulfill that plan until you can be yourself. **Success-Minded People** know that it is God's will for them to be all that they can be. Speaker and author Zig

Ziglar always said that God placed in you the seeds of greatness. It is up to you to nurture and care for that seed so it grows into all for which it was intended. He said, *"You were born to win, but to be a winner you must plan to win, prepare to win and expect to win."*

As you move forward in life *"just being:* **Your Name Here** *"* remember that you are more than okay, more than average. You are a **Success-Minded Person,** and there is greatness in you. You never can tell, you may just be the one God has chosen to change the whole program. The Scriptures tell us in the book of Jeremiah 29 that God said, *"I know the plans I have for you..."* He has it planned out and that plan is for you to succeed. You may not know all that God has in store for you, but He does. He is never caught off guard. You can trust Him and believe that He made you for something that is far better than just being okay.

"For I know the plans that I have for you, declares the Lord, plans for welfare and not for calamity to give you a future and a hope."   – Jeremiah 29:11

❧ ❧ ❧

Daily Thoughts: #3

THE BUSINESS OF THE DAY

"Let it be your business every day, in the secrecy of the inner chamber, to meet with the Holy God. You will be repaid for the trouble it may cost you. The reward will be sure and rich." — Andrew Murray

For the **Success-Minded Person**, every day is a business day. Not that you work all the time. A truly successful person has learned how to relax as well as toil. The **Success-Minded Person** works hard because their thoughts are always on their growth and success. They have a vision of what is to come, they have learned from yesterday, and they take action today. The **Success-Minded Person** knows that success is built on what they do every day.

In all the planning, action and vision, remember that the first order of business is always your relationship with the Lord. No one will find true success by allowing their relationship with God to fail. It is also not something you do when you have time. It is the first priority of the day and nothing should be done before it. How can you climb the hill of success when you have no fuel?

Take time for prayer and to read the word of God every day. This does not need to be hours, but it should be for whatever time you need it to be. Martin Luther said, *"I have so much to do today that I cannot afford to spend any less than three hours in prayer."* I realize that we cannot all spend three hours in prayer each day. I confess I do not. But the point is that it must be the time we need and it must be a priority. Schedule a quiet time with the Lord. Add it to your calendar or planner. If it means getting up an hour early, then do so. I have found that first thing in the day is best since our days get busy; and when something needs to be cut, prayer is always the first to go. Be in a place you will not be disturbed, have your Bible and focus, not on what you want from God but what God wants from you. You will soon find it to be the highlight of your day and the strength you need to succeed at all else you do.

Pastor and author, Adrian Rogers said, *"The prayer offered to God in the morning during your quiet time is the key that unlocks the door of the day. Any athlete knows that it is the start that ensures a good finish."* **Success-Minded People** know that they must start their day with power to have the fuel to achieve a powerful end. God is there, the only thing missing is you.

"Seek the Lord and His strength; seek His face continually. Remember His wonders which He has done, His marvels, and the judgments uttered by His mouth."
— Psalm 105:4–5

❧ ❧ ❧

Daily Thoughts: #4

THE GREAT RESCUE

"God just doesn't throw a life preserver to a drowning person. He goes to the bottom of the sea, and pulls a corpse from the bottom of the sea, takes him up on the bank, breathes into him the breath of life and makes him alive."

– R.C. Sproul

A strange thing happens too many of us when we become Christians. We start to think that we can still do wrong things, and God will rescue us. There are times we know that what we want to do is wrong and that we should not go down that path, but there is a voice (not God's) that tells us it is okay because Jesus will come to our rescue, He will forgive us and make it all okay again. That, my friend, is the voice of the spirit of stupid thinking talking.

Success-Minded People know that Jesus will always be there for us, even when we do stupid things, and provide forgiveness and cleansing. However, He will not ignore our sins. When we do what we know is against His word and direction for us we sin. That is called rebellion and God will not bless rebellion. Theologian Francis Schaeffer reminds us, *"The beginning of man's rebellion against God was, and is, the lack of a thankful heart."* We really do not understand or appreciate what Christ has done for us.

The lesson here is that He will not forsake you or toss you aside. But He may allow you to drown. It is good to know that He will bring you back to life, but drowning is no fun. If we struggle with sin, striving to stay faithful to Him, God will see us through and hold us up. He is always faithful. But if we deliberately sin thinking we get away with it, like Jesus is our *"get out of jail free"* card, we will find we have been sorely mistaken. C.S. Lewis said, *"There are two kinds of people: those who say to God, 'Thy will be done', and those to whom God says, 'All right, then, have it your way.'"* Which one are you?

Success-Minded People know they will never be perfect in this life. This is why we need a savior. But, those who say they are believers in Christ Jesus live to follow Him. He is not seen only as a way to escape the coming wrath, but Jesus is our Lord and Friend. Evangelist and author, Leonard Ravenhill said, *"There's a difference between changing your opinion, and changing your lifestyle."* **Success-Minded People** allow Jesus to change them and how they live. No longer do they live for themselves, but for His glory and pleasure. We live for Him because we love Him. Those who live for themselves and only call on the Name of Jesus when they are in trouble, best remember that it is a long way to the bottom.

"If we confess our sins, He is faithful and righteous to forgive us our sins and to cleanse us from all unrighteousness."
– 1 John 1:9

❖ ❖ ❖

Daily Thoughts: #5

ALWAYS AN ANSWER

"Visionary people face the same problems everyone else faces; but rather than get paralyzed by their problems, visionaries immediately commit themselves to finding a solution."

– Bill Hybles

If there is any truth I have learned over the years it is that every problem has a solution. **Success-Minded People** know that no matter how bad you think things are, there is always an answer. Of course, **Success-Minded People** also know that those answers can be very difficult to find at times.

Over the past month my wife and I have been reading about the life of Sir Ernest Shackleton. In 1914, he took a crew of 28 on his ship, the *Endurance*, to Antarctica on an expedition. Their ship was frozen in the ice and eventually crushed by the ice flow. It took two years of the most difficult conditions, but Sir Ernest made it to a distant whaling station and all 28 members were saved. It is an incredible story of leadership and bravery well worth the read.

The problems the crew of the *Endurance* faced were ones they never thought would happen. But Ernest Shackleton knew there was a way, and he only had to find it. He was known to say, *"Difficulties are just things to overcome, after all."* For those who have the confidence and willingness to persevere, they will always find the way. Why? Because there always is a way to be found.

As **Success-Minded People** go through life they will find many difficult problems in their path. Do not give up and abandon all hope. Take a new look at the problem, change your thinking and ask a better question. Then you will find the answer. As the great Albert Einstein said, *"We cannot solve our problems with the same thinking we used when we created them."* **Success-Minded People** have discovered that to change their thinking can change their life. With new, creative thinking comes new, creative answers.

If you look at problems with the understanding that the answer is out there, you will develop the confidence needed to find that answer. Your question will go from "How can I survive this?" to "How can I solve this?" The key is in how you ask the question, not if there is an answer. As author Ayn Rand said, *"The question isn't who is going to let me; it's who is going to stop me."* Once you know there is an answer, all that is left is finding it. You will be amazed how easy the answer can be when you ask the right question.

"What shall I say to these things? If God is for us, who is against us?"   — Romans 8:31

❖ ❖ ❖

Daily Thoughts: #6

EARS OPEN, MOUTH SHUT

"If you make listening and observation your occupation, you will gain much more than you can by talking."
— Robert Baden-Powell

We have all heard the old saying, *"God gave you two ears and one mouth so you should listen twice as much as you talk."* That has a great deal of truth in it. But not for the reasons you think. Many think that we should simply not talk as much as we do. The truth is that we should listen more because we can learn more by doing so.

Sir Robert Baden-Powell is not a name known to many in America. He was a great British hero from the Boer War in 1899. But what he truly did to change the world was to create the Boy Scouts in 1907. The Scouts later started in the United States in 1910, celebrating their 100th anniversary in 2010. I am a great fan of the Scouts and believe the principles that they teach young people offer an answer to the problems we face in society today.

Baden-Powell believed that by training boys to be good citizens and ready for life (the Scout motto is *Be Prepared*) they will better the world. Sir Baden-Powell said, *"A Scout is never taken by surprise; he knows exactly what to do when anything unexpected happens."* **Success-Minded People** believe that as well, but they know that it applies to all people – no matter who, or what age. We can be better people and therefore build a better society by following the Scout guidelines.

One of the greatest teachings of the Scouts is that there is much to learn and explore. It fosters a spirit of curiosity that leads to new adventures and growth in life. By simply listening and observing, you can learn so much. When you are doing the talking, you can only learn what you already know. **Success-Minded People** know that by listening, they can learn from others what they do not know and therefore grow and become better people.

Build a spirit of curiosity in yourself. Look at each person you meet and every experience you have as a learning opportunity. Treat life as what Helen Keller called *"a daring adventure."* **Success-Minded People** believe that there are so many wonderful things in the world that they do not want to miss any of them because they were striving to be heard.

> *"A wise man will hear and increase in learning, and a man of understanding will acquire wise counsel."*
>
> – Proverbs 1:5

❊ ❊ ❊

Daily Thoughts: #7

GOT A DREAM?
WRITE IT DOWN

"A #2 pencil and a dream can take you anywhere."
— Joyce Meyer

As speaker Tony Robbins says, *"Repetition is the mother of skill."* Therefore I will repeat a theme I have talked about many, many times. Here it is: When you set a goal, you must write it down. Why am I repeating this? It is because so many people just don't get it. They think that memory will work just as well. **Success-Minded People** must understand this key point: your brain leaks.

Here is the problem with memory: to start with, if you are like me you do not have one, or at least not one that works very well. A dream is only a passing thought if you cannot remember it. Also, when you try to work on something from memory, it changes each time you look at it. You get another thought, you take it in another direction. You cannot reach a destination if your road map changes each time you look at it.

Success-Minded People write down their dreams, in detail, because it helps them focus on where they are going. They know the destination, what it looks like and feels like. Writing things down gives them life. They become tangible, and you are able to hold on and look at them. In studies done on people who set goals, they have found that people who write their goals down are far more likely to reach them than those who just play it as they go.

"But I don't want to be trapped into one way," you may say. If you feel your dream is a trap, you best find a new dream. Also, writing things down does not mean they cannot be changed. **Success-Minded People** will evaluate their plans regularly and make needed adjustments to the course. You cannot do that if you do not have the course written down.

Author and entrepreneur, Gary Ryan Blair, known as "The Goals Guy," said, *"Your mind, while blessed with permanent memory, is cursed with lousy recall. Written goals provide clarity. By documenting your dreams, you must think about the process of achieving them."* The fulfillment of your dreams will not just happen. You need to work at it, and the way to start is to write it down, in detail and read it at least once a week. Once a day if you want to achieve it faster.

"Record the vision and inscribe it on tablets that the one who reads it may run. For the vision is yet for an appointed time; it hastens toward the goal, and it will not fail. Though it tarries, wait for it; for it will certainly come, it will not delay." – Habakkuk 2:2–3

❧ ❧ ❧

Daily Thoughts: #8

ACTING LIKE A GROWN-UP

"The greatest day in your life and mine is when we take total responsibility for our attitudes. That's the day we truly grow up." — Dr. John C. Maxwell

I believe by far, the biggest curse that has come upon society is that people do not take responsibility for themselves. Parents are not responsible for raising their children, people do not work because they feel the world owes them a living, and crimes are treated with therapy rather than punishment. Our social structure is collapsing, and it is all because no one wants to be responsible.

Success-Minded People know that their life is their responsibility. Do things right, and you will be blessed. Do the wrong thing, and **YOU** must deal with the consequences. Our mistakes are ours as much as our victories are. You cannot blame your folks, society, the government or God for the problems in your life. The time has come to grow-up and be responsible. It is the doorway to freedom. Singer / songwriter Bob Dylan put it this way: *"A hero is someone who understands the responsibility that comes with his freedom."*

Every day you will face responsibilities. You have a job to do or a family to care for or tasks to complete. There is no delaying responsibility, you must deal with it. President Abraham Lincoln said, *"You cannot escape the responsibilities of tomorrow by evading it today."* **Success-Minded People** know that their goals and dreams will never come to reality if they do not take full and total responsibility for them.

Responsibility is not a bad word or something to fear. The **Success-Minded Person** who takes responsibility for their life is in charge of their life. They are not at the mercy of others who want to take them places they may not want to go. Responsibility is power to the one who takes it. As Winston Churchill would say, *"The price for greatness is responsibility."*

The time has come to be an adult, to grow-up and take charge. If your life is less than what you desire for yourself, don't fuss and moan and blame others. Take responsibility for yourself and make it different. Stand up straight, take a deep breath and decide what needs to be done to make things better...then do it! This is what it means to be **Success-Minded**.

"When I was a child, I used to speak as a child, think as a child, reason as a child; when I became a man, I did away with childish things."   – 1 Corinthians 13:11

❖ ❖ ❖

Daily Thoughts: #9

FINISHING THE ASSIGNMENT

"It's not so important who starts the game but who finishes it." — Coach John Wooden

I have always been a starter. I love to start things. The problem is I have to really work at finishing. Somewhere in the process I lose interest and wander into something new. I have gotten much better at getting things done, but it takes work and focus. I have learned a lot from author and speaker David Allen who wrote the book, <u>Getting Things Done</u>. He has many great and usable tips for finishing things you start.

I also learned a great deal from a man I worked with many years ago. I was part of a team working on the opening of an IMAX Theatre. The man in charge was hired because of his history of building and opening theatres all over the world. Dave was brilliant and had the process down to the last detail. I loved working with him because you always knew what was expected and what would happen next.

Many were shocked, myself included, when right after the theatre was opened, Dave quit. See, Dave was a starter too. He loved to build theatres, but he was not interested in running one. The thing to understand is that Dave did finish the job and finished it well. He knew his strengths and worked fully in them. **Success-Minded People** know that by staying in their strengths, they will achieve more than they will by doing many different things.

Success-Minded People understand that we all have a purpose in life. There is a project that we are here to do and complete. No one is exempt. As Pastor Rick Warren, author of _The Purpose Driven Life_, said, _"If you're alive, there's a purpose for your life."_ It is that purpose that we are to finish before we leave this planet. It is that purpose that gives **Success-Minded People** their sense of fulfillment and satisfaction.

Starting is important, and I know for some that is the hard part. You must seek out your purpose, and to do that, you have to take action. David Allen gives these instructions: _"Decide the outcome and the action steps, put reminders of those somewhere your brain trusts you'll see them at the right time, and listen to your brain breathe easier."_

What do you want to do in life? God will not call you to a task that He has not given you the desire to do. Then once you start, see it through to the end. When is that end? You will know when it comes because you will be done with everything you need to do. Home is the reward for those who finish well.

> _"His Master commended him: 'Good work! You did your job well. From now on be My partner.'"_
>   – Matthew 25:21 (Message)

❖ ❖ ❖

Daily Thoughts: #10

IMAGINE THAT

"First comes thought; then organization of that thought into ideas and plans; then transformation of those plans into reality. The beginning, as you will observe, is in your imagination." — Napoleon Hill

Let's play make believe! Use your imagination and think of who you would be if all your dreams came true. How would you act? How would you talk and think? How would you treat others and be treated by them? What would you have, where would you live, how would you spend your day? Can you do this?

For many of us "adults" this common child's game is really hard to do. We have not used our imagination in a long time. That is a pity to be sure. Your imagination is extremely important. In fact, Albert Einstein, always known for his brilliant mind, said, *"Imagination is more important than knowledge."* Why is that? Isn't learning and the building of knowledge more important?

Look at the world we live in. It is just filled with wonders and technology that were only dreams a few short years ago. Where did they come from? They came from the imagination of **Success-Minded People** like you. All things start as a dream, a thought, or a wild idea in someone's mind. Motivational speaker, Brian Tracy said, *"All successful people, men and women, are big dreamers. They imagine what their future could be, ideal in every respect, and then they work every* *day toward their distant vision, that goal or purpose."* **Success-Minded People** dared to dream, to ask *"what if"* and then answered the question. Imagination is the start of all great things, and without it there is no invention.

Have you ever thought of something and one day you see it on a market shelf? You thought you could have won with that idea had you done something. You are right. The only difference between your idea and the other guys is he acted on it first. He believed in his dream and you just woke up from yours.

Take the time to pretend. Imagine what you could do and then do it. Take action and make your dreams a reality. **Success-Minded People** are going to make things better, change the world or build a better mouse trap; it might as well be you. As Donald Trump said, *"If you're going to dream anyway, you might as well dream big."*

"God can do anything, you know - far more than you could ever imagine or guess or request in your wildest dreams! He does it not by pushing us around but by working within us, His Spirit deeply and gently within us."

– Ephesians 3:20 (Message)

❋ ❋ ❋

Daily Thoughts: #11

AMAZING GRACE

"You will never cease to be the most amazed person on earth at what God has done for you on the inside."

– Oswald Chambers

John Newton who lived from 1725–1807 is best known for the hymn, <u>*Amazing Grace*</u>. The hymn was written not because he was a song writer. He was not one. It was written as a testimony of the work that God had done in Newton's life. Here is how he described himself on his own tombstone: *"John Newton, clerk, once an infidel and libertine, a servant of slaves in Africa, was, by the rich mercy of our Lord and Saviour Jesus Christ, preserved, restored, pardoned, and appointed to preach the faith he had long labored to destroy."*

John Newton was the captain of a slave ship when he came to know Christ as his personal savior. The change in Newton's life was dramatic and profound. No one was more surprised and in disbelief of the change than John Newton himself. He could not believe that God would show him, a hard, evil and rebellious man, such mercy and grace. His humble attitude toward God continued throughout his life. Near the end of his life Newton wrote, *"My memory is nearly gone, but I remember two things: That I am a great sinner, and that Christ is a great savior."*

I can relate to this as I know many other **Success-Minded People** can. No one knows the depth of sin and depravity in your heart better than you. **Success-Minded People** also know the power that is in the mercy and grace of Christ. The fact that Jesus Christ, the Son of the Living God, would die for us, even when we did not care about Him or appreciate what He did, is amazing to me. It was out of His great love for us, He willingly paid the price for our sin so we could be with Him forever.

If you do not know this power of forgiveness, I invite you to come to know Him now. You only need to confess that you are a sinner and you need His grace. Receive Jesus Christ as your personal Lord and Savior, and you too can understand the words and meaning of *"Amazing Grace / How sweet the sound / That saved a wretch like me / I once was lost / But now I'm found / Was blind but now I see."*

Success-Minded People know that there is never a full realization of success in our lives unless we have that personal relationship with God. Never be satisfied with a success that lasts only today when you can have one that lasts for eternity.

"For by grace you have been saved through faith; and that not of yourselves, it is the gift of God."

– Ephesians 2:8

❖ ❖ ❖

Daily Thoughts: #12

FREEDOM TO THINK

"The secret of living a life of excellence is merely a matter of thinking thoughts of excellence. Really, it's a matter of programming our minds with the kind of information that will set us free." — Charles R. Swindoll

American Poet and Philosopher, Ralph Waldo Emerson said, *"Life consists in what a man is thinking of all day."* Do you realize the power that is in your thoughts? If you think negative thoughts, you will have a bad day, no matter what happens that is good. If you think positive thoughts, you will have a good day, no matter what happens that is bad. Have an imaginary fight in your head and you become angry for no reason. We have all done it.

Just as when you eat junk food all the time your body will be unhealthy, so if you feed your mind junk it too will be unhealthy. TV, radio, movies, books or anything that goes into the mind can play a key role in how you feel and act. **Success-Minded People** understand that it is vital to feed your mind on positive and beneficial things all the time. **Success-Minded People** know a strong mental diet will produce a strong positive result.

Does this mean you should not watch TV or movies or listen to music? Of course not. There are things we like and do not like, and there is no one size fits all in these areas. Having said that, I believe you need to be careful in what you feed your mind. Does the music you listen to create positive feelings or depress and anger you? Do the movies you like to watch inspire you of make you feel lonely or upset? And of course there are those times we just want to be entertained. This is not rocket science. Just be aware of how the things you feed your mind cause you to react. If it is negative, change it.

When we feed our mind good positive information and entertainment, we become more creative, more productive and we are likely to inspire others. **Success-Minded People** live out the principle that what goes into your mind will come out in your life. That my friends, is a fact. If you want to be a **Success-Minded**, positive person, feed your mind successful positive things. William James said, "*Man can alter his life by altering his thinking.*" Choose the direction you want your life to go, and your thinking can make it so.

"*Finally, brethren, whatever is true, whatever is honorable, whatever is right, whatever is pure, whatever is lovely, whatever is of good repute, if there is any excellence and if anything worthy of praise, let your mind dwell on these things.*" — Philippians 4:8

❖ ❖ ❖

Daily Thoughts: #13

KEEPING GOOD COMPANY

"Associate with men of good quality if you esteem your own reputation; for it is better to be alone than in bad company."
– George Washington

When asked the question, *"How would you define a friend,"* what do you think the most common answer is? Someone you can talk to about anything? Someone who loves you unconditionally? Someone who is there for you when you need them? No, the most common answer is, someone who accepts me just as I am. But of all the answers given, that is the wrong one.

People who accept you "just the way you are" are not friends, they are called strangers. The kid at the party store, the person in the fast food drive-thru window, the clerk in the post office, they all accept you just the way you are. They don't care about you. You are just one of many faces that pass their way every day. **Success-Minded People** know that a true friend always wants to make them better than what they are. As Henry Ford said, *"My best friend is the one who brings out the best in me."*

As a **Success-Minded Person** you work to better yourself and face the many changes that requires. Of all those changes, the toughest one to make will be in the area of friends. Here is the hard cold fact: there may be friends that you need to leave behind if you plan to move forward.

That seems very hard I know, but there are those who will drag you down and work against your success.

Success-Minded People must not allow those who would kill their dreams; drain their energy and pull them down to have a place in their life. You are not rejecting your old friends; you are just not allowing them to destroy you. Think that is extreme? Look around and see how many would-be successful people have failed due to the negative influences in their life. As author John Stott said, *"Sin and the child of God are incompatible. They may occasionally meet, but they cannot live together in harmony."*

Remember that you can and should be a loyal friend to all; you do not, however, have to hand your life over to them. Be the example by doing what is right and leaving all else behind. I know it is hard, but it is the best move you will make. The example you set by being a **Success-Minded Person** will be the light that others will follow out of darkness.

"Do not be deceived: 'Bad company corrupts good morals.'."
– 1 Corinthians 15:33

❖ ❖ ❖

Daily Thoughts: #14

LIVING TODAY

"One today is worth two tomorrows."
– Benjamin Franklin

Success-Minded People often struggle with living in today. We can be so focused on our goals and the future that we miss what is going on today. While having a vision for the future is important, it is not where things happen. The future and the past have one thing in common, you cannot live there. You can only live and act in today.

In 2004, author and leadership expert Dr. John C. Maxwell published what I believe was a landmark book titled, **Today Matters**. I feel no one understands leadership and the thinking of **Success-Minded People** as much as Dr. Maxwell. *"You will never change your life until you change something you do daily."* He wrote, *"You see, success doesn't just suddenly occur one day in someone's life. For that matter, neither does failure. Each is a process. Every day of your life is merely preparation for the next. What you become is the result of what you do today."*

It is what you will do today that will bring you closer or farther away from your goal. Newspaper Editor and Pulitzer Prize-Winner, William Allen White said, *"Multitudes of people have failed to live for today. They have spent their lives reaching for the future. What they have had within their grasp today they have missed entirely, because only the future has intrigued them, and the first thing they know, the future becomes the past."*

Success-Minded People know that achievement is only possible for those who act in the present. It is good to learn from the past, and if you do not plan for the future, you will not reach your goals. But it is in the actions of today that the real victories are won. **Success-Minded People** prepare for the future by doing the right thing today, learning the right lessons and developing the right skills - today. If your life is based on what you will do, you will do nothing.

We talk a lot about planning and goal setting, but always remember that the action steps needed to achieve a goal can only be taken today. If you miss today you will never get it back. All the joy and wonders the Lord has for you to discover are within the borders of today. Do not waste a moment trying to hold on to the past; it can never change or return. Do not allow the achievements of today to be missed while you wait for a tomorrow that will never come. There is only today and today is good.

"This is the day which the Lord has made; let us rejoice and be glad in it."   – Psalm 118:24

❖ ❖ ❖

Daily Thoughts: #15

GENERATION WHATEVER

"Each generation of the church in each setting has the responsibility of communicating the gospel in understandable terms, considering the language and thought-forms of that setting." — Francis Schaeffer

The Lord led me into a life-changing discovery not too long ago. My wife and I moved on from a church we had been working at and attending for 15 years. Our job was done and we believed the Lord was calling us on to a new assignment. It was a difficult change in that we had to leave many dear people we had grown to love. But we felt it was right, so that was a comfort to us.

In the search for a new church home we visited several churches. One was a denomination that was very different to what we were accustomed. It was there we felt we were to stay for a season. What was very different, we soon found very comforting, and it ignited a new power in our relationship with the Lord. We felt we were able once again to understand holiness and reverence toward the Lord.

What I came to understand is that God in His great love for us has allowed so many different churches. People have complained that we should not have denominations because we are all one in Christ. Yes we are all one body, but we are all very different. Some feel they worship God best in a free and exciting service; others like a more traditional service. It is a wonderful thing that the Lord has allowed us all to worship from our hearts in a way that we understand and like.

Scripture tells us to seek understanding. That comes by being with like-minded people worshiping and learning in a way with which we can connect. There are things that are Biblical tenants of the faith that we all must embrace, but that does not include music or worship style or ritual. I love the quote from Mark Twain, *"It ain't those parts of the Bible that I can't understand that bother me, it is the parts that I do understand."*

Do not close yourself off to the Body of Christ just because they worship or do things differently than you. **Success-Minded People** must understand that unity in the faith is not a case of everyone being the same. Or as Dr. Martin Luther King, Jr. said, *"We may all come from different ships, but we're in the same boat now."* It is the fact that we are all sinners saved by the blood of Christ which makes us one. Be where God leads you and recognize that though it may be different for your brother or sister, it is just as good.

"Make your ear attentive to wisdom; incline your heart to understanding."   – Proverbs 2:2

❖ ❖ ❖

Daily Thoughts: #16

THE LIGHT OF DAY

"I believe in Christianity as I believe the sun has risen: not only because I see it, but because by it I see everything else."
— C.S. Lewis

Daylight is a wonderful thing if you think about it, which most of us don't. Every day the sun comes up and we have light, but we seldom ever think about the fact that we can see. It is just one of those things, like breathing, that you really don't spend time thinking about. In the light we become aware and can move about without fear of bumping into things. It is what the light shows us that we see, not the light itself.

The same is true for those who call themselves **Success-Minded Christians**. Once we have *"come into the light"* we see things in ourselves that we never before noticed. Attitudes and old habits that were always there but never noticed seem to be very noticeable now. We see this in our surroundings as well. Things that once meant nothing to us or were attractive are now bothersome and repulsive. Funny that our first reaction is that there is something wrong with us. Truth is, there is something right with us.

The Bible in the book of 1 John:1 tells us that *"God is light, and in Him there is no darkness at all."* We see the sin that is in us and the world around us because He has shed light on what was once in darkness. It has always been there, we just never saw it before. Or at least we did not see it for what it is … sin. As Henry David Thoreau said, *"It's not what you look at that matters, it's what you see."*

There is good news here as well. That same portion of Scripture in 1 John goes on to tell us that *"if we walk in the light as He Himself is in the light, we have fellowship with one another, and the blood of Jesus His Son cleanses us from all sin."* God has not revealed our sin to make us feel bad about ourselves, but to cleanse it by the sacrifice of His own Son Jesus. Evangelist, Leonard Ravenhill said, *"Our God is a consuming fire. He consumes pride, lust, materialism, and other sins."*

As a **Success-Minded Christian** enjoy the light that God has placed you in. See what is around you and be wise. Know where to walk and what to avoid. That is the advantage of light you know. Do not become judgmental or critical of those around you who may still be stumbling in the dark. You are no better, just forgiven. Help them come into the light and see what is around them as well.

> *"But the path of the righteous is like the light of dawn that shines brighter and brighter until the full day."*
> – Proverbs 4:18

❖ ❖ ❖

Daily Thoughts: #17

CHECK IT OFF THE LIST

"One of the secrets of getting more done is to make a To-Do list every day, keep it visible, and use it as a guide to action as you go through the day."

– Jean de La Fontaine

I have always been a big supporter of the simple to-do list. I make a list of everything. It keeps me organized focused and rewarded. Rewarded? Yes, I love to check things off my list. I will even add tasks that I completed that were not on the list so I can mark them off. It is like a contest against myself for how many checks I can get.

I came across a blog called **Goals & Aspiration** by Jeanne May that had a list of 5 benefits to having a to-do list. They are simple (that is the point of the list, to keep things simple) but, I feel, helpful:

1) *You do not need to rely on your memory.* **Getting Things Done** expert David Allen talks of getting the clutter out of your head. The more you keep in your memory the easier it is to get things confused. **Success-Minded People** will write things down and then rely on the list to help them, not their memory.

2) *Lists enable you to prioritize.* By doing a list you can put things in order by importance. This way important things will not fall through the cracks.

3) *You can start your day the night before.* By doing a list of tasks in the evening for the next day you can start

your day running and get things done. **Success-Minded People** know that one hour of planning can save them five in needless distractions.

4) *Make an action plan.* A list will allow you to have an action plan of what needs to be done when. It is like creating a road map to getting things done.

5) *A list can help you focus.* By having a good to-do list the **Success-Minded Person** can keep focused on the task at hand. Do not allow other things to distract you from your work. Use a good list as a guide, if it is not on the list, it can wait, and go on the next list.

Success-Minded People know that a good to-do list will not solve all their problems and simplify their work load totally, but it will make a big difference. It is a simple thing with a big impact. I have always found that a job is easier when you use the right tool. The to-do list is the perfect tool for the **Success-Minded Person** who wishes to get things done. Add it to your tool belt.

"So we built the wall and the whole wall was joined together to half its height, for the people had a mind to work."
— Nehemiah 4:6

❖ ❖ ❖

Daily Thoughts: #18

IT'S NO ACCIDENT

"Productivity is never an accident. It is always the result of a commitment to excellence, intelligent planning, and focused effort. " — Paul J. Meyer

When people come for coaching or to ask questions about their dreams and purpose, they so often say, *"I am looking for things to be right, and then I will give myself fully to my dream. "* Or *"I keep waiting for things to happen but they just don't. "* Here is a news flash: Things will never just happen! The time will never be right! If it is going to happen, **YOU** have to make it so.

One of my favorite quotes is from race car driver Mario Andretti who said, *"Desire is the key to motivation, but it's the determination and commitment to an unrelenting pursuit of your goal – a commitment to excellence – that enables you to attain the success you seek. "* **Success-Minded People** know that to achieve in any field or any area of life takes hard work. It never just happens. It is not an accident, it is very deliberate.

It is easy for people to look at the lives of **Success-Minded People** who have achieved any kind of success and see them as lucky, as if they just stumbled on their good fortune. The great industrialist Andrew Carnegie made the statement, *"The harder I work, the luckier I get. "* If you are not willing to pay the price for your success you will never have it. And there are too many who are not willing to pay that price.

This is why people play the lottery. They think they will become rich without working for it. People spend money they do not have on a game they cannot win for a fortune they do not deserve. This is not the way of the **Success-Minded Person**.

Your life has so much in store for you. You can achieve your dreams and fulfill your purpose *IF* you are willing to change and do what is needed to succeed. Attorney Kerry Randall said it clearly. *"Contrary to popular opinion, life does not get better by chance, life gets better by change. And this change always takes place inside; it is the change of thought that creates the better life."*

You are not a victim of life, no matter who you are. God has placed in you the potential to be something great. There will always be room for those **Success-Minded People** who, when given an opportunity, take it with both hands and do all they can to achieve. Those men and women who make things happen rather than wait for things to happen to them. Are you one of them? Then figure the cost, pay the price and enjoy the rewards.

"For which of you, when he wants to build a tower, does not first sit down and calculate the cost, to see if he has enough to complete it?"   – Luke 14:28

❖ ❖ ❖

Daily Thoughts: #19

ENERGY CRISIS

"The higher your energy level, the more efficient your body. The more efficient your body, the better you feel and the more you will use your talent to produce outstanding results."
— Tony Robbins

When you start to talk about health you start to step on many toes, including your own. Good health is one of those areas that we can all agree the other guy needs. When it comes to ourselves it can be a different story. Giving up unhealthy habits, losing weight, eating right and exercise are dangerous grounds, but we will cross them all the same.

Tony Robbins calls energy *"the fuel of success."* You do not want to be driving down the road of success and run out of gas. The **Success-Minded Person** must understand that health is the key to achieving their dreams. We have talked many times that success in any area is hard work; you cannot do the work if your energy level is at a low.

Health expert, A.J. Reb Materi said, *"So many people spend their health gaining wealth, and then have to spend their wealth to regain their health."* That is so true. The sad part is that keeping your health is really not that difficult a thing. **Success-Minded People** must learn to put as much commitment into their health as they do their dream.

Find a good diet and exercise plan. So which ones work? All of them. That's right, all of them. The trick is not finding a plan, it is finding a plan you will follow. We are all different so we all approach diet and exercise differently. Find something that works for you and stay with it. If it is too complicated to follow, toss it and find another. There are many to choose from.

There are a few universal rules to follow that in themselves will bring better health to you.

1) *Eat right:* Do not over eat anything. Get rid of the junk foods. Eat more fruits and veggies. Cut down on the snacks.

2) *Exercise:* This can be just a walk every day. That is a benefit in more ways than just for weight loss. Walking can help you think, is good for your heart and lungs and can be a nice break in the day.

3) *Rest:* Get some good rest every day. If possible, listen to your own clock. Are you a morning person? Get up early and go to bed early. Are you an evening person? Stay up later and get up later. If you can, try to fit into your own schedule.

"Do you not know that you are a temple of God, and that the Spirit of God dwells in you? If any man destroys the temple of God, God will destroy him, for the temple of God is holy, and that is what you are."

– 1 Corinthians 3:16–17

❖ ❖ ❖

Daily Thoughts: #20

WHO SAID IT COULDN'T BE DONE?

"It is for us to pray not for tasks equal to our powers, but for powers equal to our tasks, to go forward with a great desire forever beating at the door of our hearts as we travel towards our distant goal." – Helen Keller

Whenever someone says, *"I can't do it,"* there is always an example to show them they are wrong. There is however, no better example to everyone who says things are impossible than Helen Keller. Helen Keller (1880-1968) as a child was locked in the worst of all prisons, her own body. She was blind, deaf and mute, unable to communicate with the world around her. The chances of her growing up to be an author, political activist and lecturer were impossible. It could not be done, but she was a **Success-Minded Person** who did not accept impossible.

The story of Helen Keller has fascinated thousands, and yet I feel that many have missed the truth of her story. Rather than see Helen as someone who overcame impossible odds, see her as an example that nothing is impossible to the **Success-Minded Person**. Life offers many challenges. Oh how sad when a person facing challenges just surrenders and gives up.

Dr. John C. Maxwell said, *"You don't overcome challenges by making them smaller. You overcome them by making yourself bigger."* There was nothing Helen Keller could do to make things better. At that time there was no surgery or devices she could use. Throughout her entire life she never regained he sight or hearing. She did learn to speak and in fact was one of the top lecturers of her day.

So what happened to Helen Keller to make such a change? First, someone came into her life and helped her see that there was hope. Then she started to grow and never stopped. In her words she said, *"Life is a great adventure or nothing."* Have you seen your life as an adventure or are you willing to settle with nothing?

There are many today who are healthy, strong, with sight, hearing and full movement who are in a greater prison than Helen Keller ever was. *"It is a terrible thing,"* Helen said *"to see and have no vision."* Some people see themselves as victims of life and allow whatever happens to overtake them. There are also many more **Success-Minded People** like Helen Keller in the world. Those who have every disadvantage, every handicap and yet excel in life to enjoy success at its fullest.

Never say it cannot be done. Helen Keller proved that is not so. Be a **Success-Minded Person** by following her example and joining the great adventure. Life is far too exciting to miss.

"I can do all things through Him who strengthens me."
– Philippians 4:13

❖ ❖ ❖

Daily Thoughts: #21

DO IT AGAIN

"Excellence is an art won by training and habituation. We do not act rightly because we have virtue or excellence, but we rather have those because we have acted rightly. We are what we repeatedly do. Excellence, then, is not an act but a habit." — Aristotle

What does it take to be a **Success-Minded Person** of excellence? Is it when you do everything right every time? Excellence is not a destination. You do not hit excellence and say, *"There, now I have made it."* Then you kick back and do nothing more. Excellence does not really come from what you do but rather from who you are – a **Success-Minded Person**.

There are many talented people who can do their craft with excellence as far as the craft itself – singers, musicians, artists and writers who excel at what they do. There are those who hold high office and powerful positions. That however does not make them a **Success-Minded Person** of excellence. That comes from character. Samuel Brengle, the great Salvation Army preacher of the early 1900's said, *"The final estimate of men shows that history cares not an iota for the rank or title a man has born, or the office he has held, but only the quality of his deeds and the character of his mind and heart."*

Success-Minded People must be people of character. It is character that will keep you striving when everyone around you has given up. It is character that will help you to stand for what is right and true in spite of the opposition you face. Excellence demands that one is willing to not settle for mediocre ... ever. **Success-Minded People** know that they can do their best and will settle for nothing less. Industrialist Charles Schwab said, *"When a man has put a limit on what he will do, he has put a limit on what he can do."*

Success-Minded People of excellence know that there is a cost to success, and they are willing to do what it takes to get it. They will never do anything underhanded or dishonest, but always with integrity and dignity. They know that when they compromise integrity, they lose excellence. There is no such thing as a successful dishonest person. What seems like success today will always be followed by destruction.

Stand firm. Be a **Success-Minded Person** and give your best. Never think that success will require you to compromise your integrity. Remember the advice of Benjamin Franklin: *"A small leak can sink a great ship."* Excellence means you are at your best, all the time and getting better as you go.

"Be on alert, stand firm in the faith, act like men, be strong."   – 1 Corinthians 16:13

❖ ❖ ❖

Daily Thoughts: #22

ARE WE THERE YET?

"This life, therefore, is not righteousness but growth in righteousness, not health but healing, not being but becoming, not rest but exercise. We are not yet what we shall be, but we are growing toward it. The process is not yet finished, but it is going on. This is not the end, but it is the road. All does not yet glean in glory, but all is being purified."

– Martin Luther

There is not a parent who does not have an *"Are we there yet?"*story about their children. There are some things that are just universal, and the impatience of children is one of them. Sadly, that impatience does not go away as we become adults; it just seems to morph into something different. It is not the journey to grandma's house that we get impatient with but the journey of life.

Pastor and author of **The Purpose Driven Life**, Rick Warren said, *"Christlikeness is your eventual destination, but your journey will last a lifetime."* As believers in Jesus Christ, it is our ultimate desire for God to transform us into the image of His Son. Through prayer and Bible study we daily live as best we can to be the people God has called us to be. In the end however, we see that we fall so short of the goal.

Success-Minded People do what we can to be godly but we know that sin still contaminates our hearts. Oh, we may not get drunk, smoke or do drugs. No partying or bad behavior can be seen on the outside, but inside we have bad attitudes, negative thoughts and hearts set on the world more than on God. We plead before God to change us and wonder why we have not made sainthood yet.

Here is the good news, God has control of your life and He is making you into the person He created you to be. He knows your heart and desire to serve Him. He also knows how hard it has been. Author Max Lucado said, *'God never said the journey would be easy, but He did say the arrival would be worthwhile.'* **Success-Minded People** hold on to the promise that God will indeed make them the people He has called them to be.

Hang on my dear friend. No we are not there yet, but we will be soon enough. Trust God and follow the path he has set for you. Live for Him and you will find that you have changed more than you thought. I love what Preacher George Whitefield said, *"How sweet the rest after fatigue! How sweet will heaven be when our journey is ended."*

"Beloved, now we are children of God, and it has not appeared as yet what we shall be. We know that, when He appears, we shall be like Him, because we shall see Him just as He is." – 1 John 3:2

❖ ❖ ❖

Daily Thoughts: #23

PURPOSE

"The man who sinks his pick axe into the ground wants that stroke to mean something. The convict's stroke is not the same as the prospector's, for the obvious reason that the prospector's stroke has meaning and the convict's stroke has none. Prison is not a mere physical horror. It is using the pick axe to no purpose." – Antoine de Saint-Exupery

You have heard me say many times that we all have a purpose in life, sometimes that we were created to do and is unique to us. There are two reasons for that purpose of which the **Success-Minded Person** needs to be aware. They will help us to better understand why we are here and what we must do.

First is the plan of God. I believe that God has a plan for this world and all in it. Each of us plays a part in His master plan. Your role is important, and you are the only one who can fulfill it. It is what you were created for, and God has always intended you to perform it. He had no quota to fill, and you are not just a biological happening. God created you for His reasons.

Second is that we need a purpose. Each of us was made to do something greater than ourselves. Business leader Charles Handy said, *"In business, as in life, we all need a purpose beyond ourselves to feel useful, worthwhile and good about ourselves."* It is the lack of purpose that has been the cause of much depression and discouragement in people's lives.

When we feel we do not matter, we stop feeling we have a reason to live. The **Success-Minded Person** is someone who has come to understand and embrace their purpose.

God shows us our purpose by giving us a dream. I do not mean the dreams we have when sleeping, but the dream in your heart – that desire you have to accomplish something special, something that we feel created to do. The **Success-Minded Person** knows the pursuit of their purpose will bring fulfillment and completion to their life. There is no greater feeling than to know you are doing something that has meaning, that your life counts and the world is better because you have lived. Adding value to people and service to others is the pathway to all meaningful work.

Let me end with the words of the great Og Mandino who stated: *"I am here for a purpose and that purpose is to grow into a mountain, not to shrink to a grain of sand. Henceforth will I apply all my efforts to become the highest mountain of all and I will strain my potential until it cries for mercy."* Write this out and put it where you can read it every day. Let it be the motto you live by and you will find success in all you do.

"The Lord had made everything for its own purpose."
                                                    – Proverbs 16:4

❖ ❖ ❖

Daily Thoughts: #24

A TREASURE MAP

"All you need is a plan, the road map, and the courage to press on to your destination." – Earl Nightingale

Nothing used to stir a young boy's heart like a treasure hunt. (I believe that it still is the case, but we seem to have a shortage of imagination these days. But that is a different issue.) There was excitement following the steps of a treasure map that take you to a place where you would find riches beyond belief. For the **Success-Minded Person** the treasure is their dream.

Life can be a kind of treasure hunt. We are given a map (the Bible) and the treasure (our dream) and we can now start the hunt. It takes planning and a great deal of adventure. You will go places you never dreamed of and do things you did not think you could. It is daring and dangerous but exciting and irresistible to the **Success-Minded Person**.

You will meet pirates on the way as well. They are the negative people who will try to steal your dream. They will give you bad directions to throw you off course and say "*You can't find it. It was never really there in the first place.*" They will do all they can to drag you down and make you one of them. But **Success-Minded People** will always fight back and resist. You are the hero of this tale, and you will win.

Treasures come in many shapes and sizes. Here is how some noted hunters described their treasures:

"There is more treasure in books than in all the pirate's loot on Treasure Island." – Walt Disney

"Next to the word of God, the noble art of music is the greatest treasure in the world." – Martin Luther

"If love is the treasure, laughter is the key." – Yakov Smirnoff

"Knowledge is the treasure of a wise man." – William Penn

What is your treasure? The hunt is on, and it is out there for you to discover. Pursue your dream with all you have in your heart. Protect it from the pirates around you, and enjoy the riches it offers. The dream is waiting. It is not buried deep. Grab your map and let the adventure begin.

"By wisdom a house is built, and by understanding it is established; and by knowledge the rooms are filled with all precious and pleasant riches."   – Proverbs 24:3-4

❖ ❖ ❖

Daily Thoughts: #25

YES YOU CAN!

"That some achieve great success, is proof to all that others can achieve it as well." — Abraham Lincoln

We have all heard some successful person say, *"If I can do it so can you."* While I do agree with that statement, I feel it is incomplete and a bit misleading. The full statement should be, *"I worked hard and did what needed to be done to get the results I got. If you are willing to do the same you can get the same results."* Success is available to everyone, if you are willing to do what successful people do.

Success-Minded People know there are no short cuts on the road to success. I have often had issues with those who tell people they can be successful at something (no matter what it is) in their spare time. It never works that way. Yes, there are many opportunities out there that will offer success, and you can meet the people who have done it. What you do not find is someone who did it in their spare time. Success takes work, full-time work.

The fact that others have had success does show that you too can succeed; however, you have got to remember that it did not just happen to them. Businessman Arnold H. Glasow said, *"Success isn't a result of spontaneous combustion. You must set yourself on fire."* Others can make a way for you to follow. You can learn from their mistakes and their successes, but they cannot do it for you. Your success is up to you as their success was up to them.

Success-Minded People know that there are many universal principles that they can and must follow to succeed at anything. These are things like a positive attitude, service to others, integrity, hard work, a teachable spirit, a desire to learn, and belief that you can succeed. Architect Frank Lloyd Wright said, *"The thing always happens that you really believe in; and the belief in a thing makes it happen."* You will find these principles in every truly **Success-Minded Person**.

The details for your particular dream are there too. Find someone who succeeded in doing what you desire to achieve. Learn what they did and do the same, minus the mistakes, of course. Hang out with positive **Success-Minded People**. Pay attention to what they say and do. The success you see in others can be yours if you learn and trust in the lessons, if you have the dream, that potential to achieve it is there in you. You only have to bring it out and live the dream.

> *"For I am confident of this very thing, that He who began a good work in you will perfect it until the day of Christ Jesus."* — Philippians 1:6

❖ ❖ ❖

Daily Thoughts: #26

BE PREPARED!

"To each there comes in their lifetime a special moment when they are figuratively tapped on the shoulder and offered the chance to do a very special thing, unique to them and fitting their talents. What a tragedy if that moment finds them unprepared or unqualified for that which could have been their finest hour."   – Sir Winston Churchill

We are all familiar with the saying, *"Be Prepared"* as the Boy Scout motto, but as with many familiar things we pay little attention to the meaning. To be prepared is the foundation for the **Success-Minded Person**. Preparedness is what it takes to make it through the twists and turns of business or life in general. If we are not prepared for what will come our way, we will be caught in the trap of spending far too much time and energy on things. Believe me; the problems of life will come your way.

So how do you become prepared? What do you need to know? First and foremost you have to be willing to learn. By having a teachable spirit that is willing to listen, learn and follow directions from others, you can be ready for almost anything. Keep your eyes open and your mouth shut. Ask more questions than you answer, and deliberately learn something new every day. For the **Success-Minded Person**, life is a classroom and the potential for learning is endless.

You also need to know and understand your strengths. I suggest that you do a **DISC** assessment if you have not already done one. This will show your behavioral style and help you understand why you do what you do and how you best communicate with the world around you. **DISC** is a valuable tool that can help you see where you are strong and where you are not.

Success-Minded People understand their strengths, work on them, building them up and staying within them. They do not focus on their weaknesses. We are often mistakenly told to find our weakness and make it strong. That is wrong thinking. Weaknesses make us weak; it is strengths that make us strong. The **Success-Minded Person** would rather put their time and energy into going from good to great rather than from bad to okay.

Take the things you learn and put them into practice. Spend time thinking of how to handle situations that you may come across. Be ready for anything. The more prepared you are, the more confidence you will feel and the more value you will provide to all around you.

"Preach the word; be ready in season and out of season; reprove, rebuke, exhort, with great patience and instruction."
– 2 Timothy 4:2

❖ ❖ ❖

Daily Thoughts: #27

IF IT'S TRUE, IT APPLIES TO YOU

"If you don't live it, you don't believe it."

– Paul Harvey

I have a 6-year-old grandson who is at the stage where he seems to know everything. If you try to show him something, his first response is *"I know that."* It's cute in a 6-year-old, but I also know many adults who tell me that. I meet them when I speak or train, and they feel they must let me know that they already knew the information I told them. There is nothing about successful living they do not already know.

So, do they live the success they feel they know so well? No. Have they put the principles into play in their life? No. I know that I myself have a great deal to learn in life, but I have grabbed this truth: if you say you believe something and do not live by it, you are only kidding yourself. **Success-Minded People** know that they will never learn all there is to know. Leadership expert John C. Maxwell said, *"It's one thing to believe that you possess remarkable potential. It's another thing to have enough faith in yourself that you think you can fulfill it."*

I can tell you over and over again that you can succeed in achieving your dream, and you can say you believe it. But if you never do anything to move in that direction, your belief is empty and meaningless. Head knowledge is of little value if there is never any action to follow it up. The whole point of talking about being a **Success-Minded Person** is so that you will take these principles and live them.

Success-Minded People have an awakening at some point. They realize that they have missed something in life and they begin to build a hunger for it. The something they are missing is action and results. Phillips Brooks, who wrote the Christmas hymn, O Little Town of Bethlehem, said, *"When you discover you've been living only half a life, the other half is going to haunt you until you develop it."* **Success-Minded People** know that with knowledge there must be action.

Take the truth you know, and apply it to your life. It can be in business, church, your personal or spiritual life, it does not matter. If you believe it to be true, live it. Even if you are just hopeful that the principles are true, live them out and see for yourself. To take the time to learn something new and then never really put it into play in your life is such a sad waste of time. **Success-Minded People** have the power to change their whole life. It only takes some action and a bit of believing.

"Take pains with these things; be absorbed in them, so that your progress may be evident to all."   – 1 Timothy 4:15

❖ ❖ ❖

Daily Thoughts: #28

RESPONSIBLITY

"We must reject the idea that every time a law's broken, society is guilty rather than the lawbreaker. It is time to restore the American precept that each individual is accountable for his actions." – Ronald Reagan

There are two things that drive me crazy. One is political correctness, and the other is the lack of responsibility we have in our society today. **Success-Minded People** must realize that they will never reach a level of true success unless they take full responsibility for their life. As speaker, Les Brown said, *"Accept responsibility for your life. Know that it is you who will get you where you want to go, no one else."*

What personal responsibility means is to take control of your life, to realize that what you do and where you go is a matter of choice, and you are the one making the choice. **Success-Minded People** know that if things happen, good and bad, they must be responsible for them. Author and leadership trainer, Jim Rohn, said, *"You must take personal responsibility. You cannot change circumstances, the seasons, or the wind, but you can change yourself. That is something you have charge of."*

If there are addictions or bad habits that you need to overcome in your life, you must first take the responsibility for them. You cannot blame your parents, your spouse or society. Your choices are your own. Once you take responsibility you can make the changes needed because you are in charge again. Those who hide behind excuses for their bad behavior will never see victory in life. As Benjamin Franklin said, *"He who is good at excuses is good at very little else."*

The same is true for the success in your life. **Success-Minded People** work hard to make the right choices and do the right things. That is responsibility. It is not just owning up to mistakes, it is also, and mainly, making choices. I love the books by Dr. Seuss. I read them when I was a kid, and I read them to my grandchildren. In his book, **Oh, The Places You Will Go**, he said: *"You have brains in your head. / You have feet in your shoes. / You can steer yourself / Any direction you choose."*

Success-Minded People will take responsibility for themselves and know they will never live successfully until they face it, embrace it and enjoy the reality of it. It feels good to be in charge of yourself.

"But let each one examine his own work, and then he will have reason for boasting in regard to himself alone, and not in regard to another. For each one shall bear his own load." – Galatians 6:4–5

❧ ❧ ❧

Daily Thoughts: #29

NO DOUBT

"The only thing that will guarantee the successful conclusion of a doubtful undertaking is faith in the beginning that you can do it." — William James

Stubbornness is not what you would usually see as a good quality. When it is part of the character of the **Success-Minded Person** I guess we would call it determination. But the truth is you are stubborn. You will not give up. Why? Because you believe in what you are doing.

A **Success-Minded Person** has a strong belief in their dream or purpose, and that is vital to full success in anything. Talk to **Success-Minded People** who have achieved what some would call the impossible, and they will tell you that they believed they could do it all along. Not allowing doubts or fears to get control, they knew what had to be done, believed in what they were doing and did it.

Dale Carnegie said, *"Inaction breeds doubts and fear. Action breeds confidence and courage. If you want to conquer fear, do not sit at home and think about it. Go out and get busy."* Action is the most powerful ingredient in the success formula. Too many people just talk about success, or just think about success or even just plan for success. Successful people actually go out and do success.

As a **Success-Minded Person** believes in his or her dream or purpose he/she seems to be able to build a power to do what he/she may not do otherwise. A **Success-Minded**

Person knows that it can be done and is totally convinced that he or she cannot fail. Walt Disney, a man who believed the impossible and that he could do what others said he could not, built his fantasy kingdom in an old orange grove. Disney had a dream, he believed in that dream, and took action and there was Disneyland.

What is your Disneyland? What is the dream you have that may seem too big for even you to believe in? Do not allow others to steal it from you or tell you that you cannot have it. Believe in the dream and then take action. Understand that it is in taking action that you will see it all come to reality. You don't need the details first; start with what you have. Take a first step and then the next. It will all come. The money, the people, the knowledge, it will all come.

I believe in you. My action is writing things of encouragement and direction. Someone who is reading this will be the **Success-Minded Person** who will make the world better. They have the idea that will change it all or the product that will make millions of lives better. This is my dream and I have no doubt that it will happen and is happening.

"And Jesus said to him, 'If you can! All things are possible to him who believes." – Mark 9:23

❖ ❖ ❖

Daily Thoughts: #30

TIME TO SAY GOODBYE

"We want something new but cannot let go of the old-old ideas, beliefs, habits, even thoughts. We are out of contact with our own genius. Sometimes we know we are stuck; sometimes we don't. In both cases we have to do something."
— Rush Limbaugh

I remember reading about some tribal group of people who had a unique approach to punishment for murder. If someone was guilty of taking another's life without a cause, the punishment was that the body of the dead was tied to the murderer, and they had to carry it around with them for the rest of their life. How is that for a deterrent to crime?

That is the way some believers in Christ are when it comes to their old life. Scripture tells us the old man (our old nature) is dead. But we do not allow him to be buried and put out of sight. We hold on to the past like it was some treasure we do not wish to lose. We keep going back to old habits, old friends, and old ways of living. We just do not move on.

When we give our life to Christ, we become new. One of my favorite verses is 2 Corinthians 5:17. It tells me that my past, the old me, is gone. I do not have to drag it around anymore. I do not have to fear it, struggle with it or hide it from others. It is gone and the new me is in its place. I am not the person I was before. All the additions and bad habits are gone. I feel, think and behave differently than I did.

Even my passions and desires have changed from focused on me to Him. While in Ireland a few years back I saw the grave of a 17th century Nun which read, *"I am His. And His I choose to be."* That is my heart. I am the property of Jesus, and I have no desire for anything else.

"But what about your dream to help people become the best they can be and to achieve their dreams? What of all you say about goal setting and fulfilling your purpose?" You see, that all is part of it. I know that to be a **Success-Minded Person** and fully serve God, as I desire to do, I have a responsibility to be who He created me to be. J. Oswald Sanders, author of **Spiritual Leadership** said, *"All Christians are called to develop God-given talents, to make the most of their lives, to develop to the fullest their God-given powers and capacities."*

God made each of us for a purpose. No one is here by mistake. Our duty and honor to the Creator is to be the best creation we can be. As a **Success-Minded Christian** you will not just finish what God has for you to do, but you will do it well.

"Therefore if any man is in Christ, he is a new creature; the old things passed away; behold, new things have come."
— 2 Corinthians 5:17

❄ ❄ ❄

Daily Thoughts: #31

REDISCOVERING LIFE

"There is frequently more to be learned from the unexpected questions of a child than the discourses of men."
— John Locke

I have always said that the one thing I liked doing best was being a Dad. I loved every minute of raising my daughters. They have always been, and still are, the light of my life. Now that they have grown, it has gotten better – it's called grandchildren. As of this writing, there are seven. My wife and I cannot get enough of them. Children are like discovering the world all over again, and each has their own perspective.

One of my heroes in life has been Mr. Rogers. Every morning I would sing, *"It's a lovely day in the neighborhood..."* to my girls (they hated it). To this day I have a picture of Fred Rogers on my bookshelf. Fred Rogers understood that grown-ups had as much to learn from children as the children did from grow-ups. He would say, *"You know, you don't have to look like everybody else to be accepted and to feel accepted."* A lesson all **Success-Minded People** need to know.

Another person who taught great lessons to children as well as adults was Dr. Seuss. He said, *"Think left and think right and think low and think high. Oh, the things you can think up if you only try."* This is a great principle of life. If you did not read to your children, you would have missed that.

Sadly, some who read still miss it anyway thinking it is for kids.

Children can offer you a great education if you will pay attention. As adults, we work so hard to teach them to be like us, when if we were really wise, we would learn to be more like them. There is a reason that Jesus said we were to be like little children. Children can believe the impossible with little effort. They are told they can be anything, and they believe it. It is not till they start to grow, and we tell them they must be reasonable that they start to limit themselves.

Spend time with children and purposely learn from them. Stop being the *"grown-up"* for a while and play with them, allowing them to teach you. Fred Rogers always said, *"Play is really the work of childhood."* The world is full of wonder; the **Success-Minded Person** can rediscover it all from the eyes and thoughts of a child.

"Truly I say to you, whoever does not receive the kingdom of God like a child shall not enter it at all." – Luke 18:17

❖ ❖ ❖

Daily Thoughts: #32

WHERE ARE THE HEROES?

"Not to walk in the straight and narrow way yourself is to give the devil the biggest kind of a chance to get our children." — Billy Sunday

I am so grateful that I got to grow up in a time when heroes were a strong part of a child's life. We had Davy Crocket, Roy Rogers, John Wayne, Neil Armstrong and many others. The things they had in common was their courage, their sense of right and a wholesome life. We wanted to be like them and knew that meant living right and standing up for what is right.

Since the 60's too many heroes became known for their rebellion and wild lives. Rock and movie stars replaced those who did brave deeds and made life better. Young people gave up wanting to be doctors, astronauts, explorers and inventors to be rappers, rock stars and criminals. The desire to be good and stand for right was replaced with the desire to be wild and rebellious.

The great writer and thinker, C.S. Lewis said, *"We are what we believe we are."* Too many people believe they are victims and outcasts in the world. They believe they must rebel in order to achieve anything. That is why so many are unhappy, unproductive and lost. In their mind they are nothing, and therefore, stand for nothing. They give real meaning to the words of Dr. Martin Luther King, Jr. who said, *"If a man hasn't discovered something that he will die for, he isn't fit to live."*

God has created each of us to be something great. The late humorist Erma Bombeck advised, *"Don't confuse fame with success. Madonna is one; Helen Keller is the other."* The world is filled with true heroes that you can follow and use as an example.

The **Success-Minded Person** knows that the greatest example of a true hero is you. They know that you do not have to invent something great, you have to be something great. You do not have to fight a war, you just have to stand for what is right. Your example will inspire others and will make you a hero in their eyes. As Dr. Billy Graham said, *"Courage is contagious. When a brave man takes a stand, the spines of others are often stiffened."*

You owe it to your children, your friends and the world to be a true hero. Follow the principles of **Success-Minded People**. It may sound simple but I dare you to try it. Old-fashioned? Doing what is right is never out of date. Being a hero will bring you to life. It gives you purpose and a sense of destiny. Life has meaning and you feel the power that is given by God to all who seek to live right.

> *"The memory of the righteous is blessed, but the name of the wicked will rot."*   – Proverbs 10:7

❖ ❖ ❖

Daily Thoughts: #33

TIME TO WAKE UP

"Some men dream of worthy accomplishments, while others stay awake and do them." — Unknown

We have all heard the sales pitch. *"You can make millions in your spare time."* That on a part-time basis, you can make enough money to retire at 40. Here is the news flash – it is not true. No one knows that better than those who bought into it and found that they still have not gained anything.

Can people in multi-level marketing or direct sales (those who use this line the most) make money? They can make millions. You can succeed and the money is there. What you cannot do is succeed in your spare time. Success takes work, full time, and hard work. **Success-Minded People** know that there is a price to pay for success and unless you are willing to pay that price you will not reap the fruits of success.

It is a lazy mindset that attracts people to the idea of easy money. They are unwilling to work and put forth the effort to succeed, so they play the lottery or find a get-rich-quick scheme thinking that there is easy money to be found. There is no easy money. No free lunch. As Thomas J. Watson, former president of IBM said, *"If you want to be a big company tomorrow, you have to start acting like one today."*

Success-Minded People are those who know their dreams and are willing to take action to achieve them.

Artist, Pablo Picasso said, *"Action is the foundational key to all success."* Nothing happens without action. Once action stops, so does success. This is why the idea of retirement is so dangerous. Oh, I just stepped on a lot of toes with that one. This is a topic for another time, but let me say that when we stop working – we stop. Man was not created to be useless. We were made for action.

Stop looking for the easy way. People who are not achievers try to find that easiest way to success, and they never seem to find the happiness they seek in life. Be a **Success-Minded Person**, roll up your sleeves and get to work. Hard work gives us a feeling of achievement, confidence and we are significant. When we have earned our success, the rewards are sweeter, we hold them with higher value, and we enjoy the self-respect of a person who reaches a goal on his or her own. Success always tastes sweeter when made by our own hands.

> *"He who gathers in summer is a son who acts wisely, but he who sleeps in harvest is a son who acts shamefully."*
> – Proverbs 10:5

❖ ❖ ❖

Daily Thoughts: #34

MEMORIES VS. DREAMS

"Never let your memories be greater than your dreams."
— Doug Ivester

Success-Minded People know that the greatest enemy to today's success is yesterday's success. What do I mean by that? Well for many, they are willing to strive and work to succeed, but once their success comes, they stop trying. You cannot live off past success. Once you stop striving, you start to go backwards. You never stand still. As IBM's Thomas J. Watson said, *"Whenever an individual or a business decides that success has been attained, progress stops."*

This is why vision is so important to the **Success-Minded Person**. They look beyond the current goal and see the long term. Author J. Oswald Sanders stated, *"Eyes that look are common; eyes that see are rare."* Too many people just want to get the goal achieved, the job done. They think that once they have finished, it is over and they can relax. **Success-Minded People** see that the job is never done. Today's success is the stepping stone for tomorrow's success.

It is when we have a dream that is bigger than what we can achieve, that we have the greatest success. **Success-Minded People** believe that God has created them for a life-time of success, not just for an event. You can see them as they go from one achievement to another. It is the goal that gives them life and moves them on. Speaker and entrepreneur, Jim Rohn tells us, *"If you go to work on your goals, your goals will go to work on you. If you go to work on your plan, your plan will go to work on you. Whatever good things we build, end up building us."*

Do not allow your thoughts of what was, steal what can be. You cannot recapture the past, even the good parts. What was yesterday's victory is only today's memory, nothing more. As a **Success-Minded Person** you must always be looking to the next victory, the next goal. Feed on the energy and the excitement of the adventure. It is not just keeping busy, it's achieving something. Athlete Bill Copeland said, *"You've removed most of the roadblocks to success when you know the difference between motion and direction."*

There is a simple success formula that **Success-Minded People** must follow: Learn from the past, and leave it behind. Plan for the future, and keep the vision clear. Live today, and make it happen. The past is a memory, the future is a dream, but today there is action.

"The plans of the diligent lead surely to advantage, but everyone who is hasty comes surely to poverty."
                                                              – Proverbs 21:5

❖ ❖ ❖

Daily Thoughts: #35

SPECIAL GIFTS

"The giftedness is usually greater than the person."
                                                    – Fred Smith

I am sometimes amazed by how many people believe they do not have talent. I think the problem is how we define talent. It is not just musical ability, or the arts or a skill. Skills can be learned, but talent is inborn. We all have an ability to do something better than others. You may not see it as talent, but it is.

Leadership expert Dr. John C. Maxwell put it this way: *"People have equal value, but not equal giftedness. Some people seem to be blessed with a multitude of talents. Most of us have fewer abilities. But know this: all of us have something that we can do well."* What is even more important is for you to understand that your talents are needed by the rest of the world. God did not place you here to fill a space; you have a work to do that is part of His great plan for mankind.

Success-Minded People come to understand two important realities. One is that they have a gift, a talent to give. Two is that others are also talented and have value. I like how Coach John Wooden put it: *"Talent is God-given. Be humble. Fame is man-given. Be grateful. Conceit is self-given. Be careful."* You should use and celebrate your talents, but do not think you are the end all in giftedness.

Success-Minded People also must understand that talent alone is not enough. You have to be able to use your talents to add value to others, not just to impress yourself. The person who is greatly talented and does nothing is an old story. Many failures in life have been highly gifted people. You must use your talents, develop them and improve them in order to succeed.

Mary Kay Ash, founder of the Mary Kay Cosmetics saw the need for women to develop their talents. She knew that every person had talent, and all they needed was the avenue to build on that. She also knew that talent was not enough for success; you had to do something about it. She said, *"Those who are blessed with the most talent don't necessarily outperform everyone else. It's the people with follow-through who excel."*

As a **Success-Minded Person,** you need to identify your talents. Do not look at what you cannot do; look at what you do well. Once you find that, you build on it. Don't under-estimate yourself or your abilities. Do not limit how you define talent. Even the great Albert Einstein understood this when he said, *"I have no special talent. I am only passionately curious."*

"A man's gift makes room for him, and brings him before great men."   – Proverbs 18:16

❖ ❖ ❖

Daily Thoughts: #36

THE BEST

"No matter the size of the bottle, the cream always rises to the top." — Charles Wilson

One of the many great qualities of a **Success-Minded Person** is that they are the best of the best. Not that they are better than everyone else, but they hold excellence to a high standard and try their best. Historian Charles Kendall Adams put it this way, *"No one ever attains very eminent success by simply doing what is required of him; it is the amount of excellence of what is over and above the required that determines greatness."*

Success-Minded People know that they will never really be great at what they do if they only do what is required of them. At work, church or in your personal life, if all you do is what is expected of you, then you cheat yourself and others of your best. A great job happens when you see what you have to do and ask yourself, *"How can I do a bit more and make this an excellent job?"*

People too often see a job as what they are paid to do. They then are surprised when their employer does not give them a raise or a promotion they are expecting. When you do only what you are paid to do, you do not bring extra value to the job. You see, they could always pay someone else and get the same job done.

Success-Minded People know that it is the extra that gives them value. Their employer knows that this person will do a good job and more. They will not get the same high quality work from someone else. This is why the **Success-Minded Person** will get the raise or promotion, because they have earned it. Never be fooled into thinking that longevity or dependability are reasons for you to get a raise or promotion. If you only do what is expected, you will get no more than what is expected. Do more – get more.

As a **Success-Minded Person** you also understand that to do more than expected, to be excellent at what you do, makes you feel better as well. Pastor and Author Bill Hybels said, *"Most people feel best about themselves when they have given their very best."* It is a fact, if you want to feel your best, do your best. There is great personal power and confidence in knowing that you are above the crowd. You may not be better than anyone else, but you know you can do better than anyone else.

"Seeing that His divine power has granted to us everything pertaining to life and godliness, through the true knowledge of Him who called us by His own glory and excellence."
                                                                    – 2 Peter 1:3

❖ ❖ ❖

Daily Thoughts: #37

THE WORK IS NEVER DONE

"The toughest thing about success is that you've got to keep on being a success. Talent is only a starting point in business. You've got to keep working that talent."

– Irving Berlin

Have you ever wanted something just to be over – finish the task and get it done and out of the way? I have many times. This is usually because we are doing something that is not in our strength set or that is not directly leading us to the achievement of a bigger goal. Those are tasks that need to be done, and there is nothing wrong with wanting them done.

Success-Minded People know that when it comes to our dreams and the achievement of our life's purpose that the job is never done. We go from one goal to another. As long as we have breath we have something to do, to improve or to conquer. I know that even **Success-Minded People** get tired and have days we feel less driven than others. You know you must go on and do what you need to. As NBA Coach Jerry West said, *"You can't get much done in life if you only work on the days you feel good."*

So what is the secret of getting things done that you do not feel like doing? To be a **Success-Minded Person** you must remember that the goal is not to finish the job; it is to achieve the outcome. Success is not a destination that you arrive at and that is it. Success, true success in life, is an ongoing process that you work at every day. You are always moving forward and always getting better. It means change and not staying the same. Author and success expert Max DePree said, *"We cannot become what we need to be by remaining what we are."*

I know that it can get hard, and we all get tired, but you cannot give in and surrender to tiredness. Diplomat Robert Strauss had it right when he said, *"Success is a little like wrestling a gorilla. You don't quit when you're tired – you quit when the gorilla is tired."* **Success-Minded People** know what wrestling that gorilla is like. But they also know what the victory is like. They know that today I may be tired, but tomorrow I may see a victory that will recharge me to move forward.

Life is filled with ups and downs. But for the **Success-Minded Person** there are far more ups than downs. That is because they have something they are working for, a dream that is before them, and they will do all they can to achieve that dream. They feel the call of God and they know that when their task on earth is done, they will rest. And the reward waiting for them is worth it all. The words they long to hear are, *"Well done, good and faithful servant."*

> *"From everyone who has been given much, much will be required; and to whom they entrusted much, of him they will ask all the more."*   – Luke 12:48

❖ ❖ ❖

Daily Thoughts: #38

CLAIMING YOUR DESTINY

"Destiny is not a matter of chance, it is a matter of choice; it is not a thing to be waited for, it is a thing to be achieved."
— William Jennings Bryan

Destiny is often misunderstood. It holds a mystery to it, like a power you cannot fight. It seems as though it is a force that sucks you in, and there is little you can do about it. That is not truly what destiny is. I believe we all have a destiny to fulfill that is given to us by God, life's purpose that we were created to do. But I also believe in free will and that we have a choice as to where our life will lead us.

Success-Minded People believe in destiny. We can call it purpose, a dream, a goal or whatever. But we know it is the thing we are created to do, and we will never feel complete until we are doing it. To follow our destiny, however, is a choice we make, not something that is thrust upon us. Reality is that many people have lived and died without fulfilling their purpose in life. They did not take control, and therefore, they did not live. As Jack Welch, former CEO of GE said, *"Control your destiny or someone else will."*

As a **Success-Minded Person** you know what you are here to do. You feel the fire burning in your soul and you cannot escape it. You want this enough that you will do what you must to achieve it. **Success-Minded People** know that just because they know their destiny does not mean they will fulfill it automatically. You have to work at it. Your attitude toward your dream must be like that of Hannibal, *"We will either find a way or make one."*

Destiny demands that we make a choice to follow it or to allow others to lead us. It takes courage and determination to achieve your destiny in life. That is why you must hold the mindset of a **Success-Minded Person**. As author and English clergyman Sydney Smith said, *"A great deal of talent is lost to the world for want of a little courage."*

Do not think that you are under the control of some other person or government or church. You are given a dream because God intended for you to fulfill it. He is aware of the limits you see and expects you to fight for your destiny. *"Victory is always possible,"* wrote Napoleon Hill, *"for the person who refuses to stop fighting."* Keep working and doing what you know you must to achieve the dream. Victory will be yours if you stay the course and fix your eyes and heart on the goal. It is your destiny!

> *"Brethren, I do not regard myself as having laid hold of it yet; but one thing I do: forgetting what lies behind and reaching forward to what lies ahead, I press on toward the goal for the prize of the upward call of God in Christ Jesus."* – Philippians 3:13–14

❖ ❖ ❖

Daily Thoughts: #39

GET OUT AND RIDE

"Life is a ten-speed bike. Most of us have gears we never use." — Charles Schulz

In 1975 film maker George Lucas got the idea for a new movie. It would require him to stretch his imagination farther than ever before. In 1977 he released the movie *Star Wars* with some of the most advanced and amazing visual effects ever seem in a film. When asked about this amazing film he said, *"The trick was learning the difference between the impossible and the merely never-before-done-or-imagined."* The biggest obstacle he faced was simply that what he wanted to do had not been done before.

Success-Minded People always have to face the never-done-before question. We are big thinkers and have great imaginations. Sadly we live in a world that tells us that impossible things cannot be done. All you have to do is look around to see that the impossible is done all the time. But there are still those who say they cannot achieve their dreams because of money, time, responsibilities or the fact that it is impossible. Inventor George Washington Carver said, *"Ninety-nine percent of failures come from people who have the habit of making excuses."*

Success-Minded People are always amazing themselves and others by achieving the impossible. In fact, it is a habit of the **Success-Minded Person** to purposely look for the impossible. We just cannot help ourselves. There is an excitement that happens when we do what we are told cannot be done. We believe the words of baseball great Sam Ewing who said, *"Nothing is so embarrassing as watching someone do something that you said could not be done."* **Success-Minded People** do not mind embarrassing others in that way.

Stop believing those who tell you that your dream is impractical or impossible. If you can dream it you can do it. Is it going to be easy? No, most likely not. Is it going to take a lot of work? You can bet on that. I love the old saying from the U.S. Marine Corps, *"The difficult we can do right now, the impossible will take a little longer."* You do not know the power you hold. You can do far more than you ever thought possible.

Success-Minded People also believe that others can do the impossible and will encourage and promote the dreams of those around them. Poet, John Andrew Holmes said, *"Never tell a young person that something cannot be done. God may have been waiting centuries for somebody ignorant enough of the impossible to do that thing."* You do not know who the person is who will change the world by doing the impossible. It may be that young person in your life. It may be you.

"...With people this is impossible, but with God all things are possible." – Matthew 19:26

❈ ❈ ❈

Daily Thoughts: #40

THE PURPOSE
OF LEARNING

"You can claim to be surprised once; after that, you're unprepared."   – Old Saying

We are all familiar with the Boy Scout motto: *Be Prepared.* But what does that mean? Boy Scout founder, Sir Robert Baden-Powell said: *"Be Prepared … the meaning of the motto is that a Scout must prepare himself by previously thinking out and practicing how to act on any accident or emergency so that he is never taken by surprise."* In short, be ready for anything because anything could happen.

One of the characteristics of a **Success-Minded Person** is that they are forever learning. For them, life is one great classroom. They see every event, every person they meet as an opportunity to learn something new. Why is learning so important? Because you never know when you will need the knowledge. Lessons are not learned to fill an empty space in your head. You learn so you can use what you learn in everyday life.

Success-Minded People know that learning and preparing is not just for when bad things happen. Yes it is good to know how to handle a crisis before it happens and to be able to solve problems as they come. But life is more than difficult times. What happens when you win? What will do when you have succeeded in your goal? Author H. Jackson Brown, Jr. had it right when he said, *"I never expect to lose. Even when I'm the underdog, I still prepare a victory speech."*

To be prepared is to be ready for whatever life brings your way. Scripture tells us to use things like wisdom, understanding and knowledge. Use them for what? Well, by learning all we can, we are ready for the battles that are ahead. We are not taken by surprise when things fall apart or when they all come together. We are ready for life, and what we don't know, we trust God to show us. As football Hall of Fame member Joe Namath said, *"First, I prepare. Then I have faith."*

Preparing by learning means that you use the tools God has put in your way. **Success-Minded People** learn by taking classes, reading books, listening to CDs and DVDs. They take any opportunity they can find to better themselves and to learn useful information. Every person who is reading this has more resources available to them, right now, than Benjamin Franklin had during his whole lifetime. Do not waste those resources. Be ready to win. Learn all you can from every source you can. Get wisdom, understanding and knowledge, and you will *Be Prepared* for anything.

"Make your ear attentive to wisdom; incline your heart to understanding."   – Proverbs 2:2

❈ ❈ ❈

Daily Thoughts: #41

GOOD SELECTIVE HEARING

"Don't listen to those who say, 'It's not done that way.'
Maybe it's not, but maybe you'll do it anyway. Don't
listen to those who say, 'You're taking too big a chance.'
Michelangelo would have painted the Sistine floor, and it
would surely be rubbed out today."　　— Neil Simon

Doesn't it make you wonder about the human heart
when we live in a day that you can talk to people
all over the world from a small cell phone, we have
been to the moon, transplanted organs, have computers
small enough to put on a pin, and yet we do not believe
people can accomplish their dreams? I will be honest
with you, I do not believe people think a dream cannot
be accomplished; I believe they don't want to see them
accomplished.

There are people in our lives who are very threatened
by our success. You see, if you achieve you dream, they will
have to achieve theirs, or at least be challenged to. This
is not a new problem; it is as old as mankind itself. Thomas Fuller, Chaplain to King Charles II of England in the
17th century, wrote, *"The real difference between men is energy.*
A strong will, a settled purpose, and invincible determination can
accomplish almost anything; and in this lies the distinction between
great men and little men."

Success-Minded People must be cautious to whom they
listen. Do not allow those who are too lazy or fearful to

accomplish their own dreams to stop you from achieving yours. Listen to those who believe in you and the fact that you can do anything God has called you to do. Listen to God, who tells us we can do all things through Christ Jesus. If He has given us a dream, He intended us to accomplish it. End of story, no excuses, and no retractions.

Success-Minded People are big thinkers. They are possibility thinkers who believe that they and others can do great things. Professor and author David J. Schwartz said, *"Big thinkers are specialists in creating positive forward-looking, optimistic pictures in their own minds and in the minds of others."* **Success-Minded People** do not hope that great things can be done - they believe it with all that is in them. They believe it so much that they never give up trying to see it happen.

If you need some encouragement in believing your dreams can come to be, search the Scriptures. No one is more encouraging, and no one believes in you more than God does. He believed in you so much that He sent His Son Jesus to die for you so you could fulfill your dreams. With God behind us, how can we ever fail?

"Every good thing given and every perfect gift is from above, coming down from the Father of lights, with Whom there is no variation or shifting shadow."   – James 1:17

❖ ❖ ❖

Daily Thoughts: #42

REMOVING THE LIMITS

"The only limit to our realization of tomorrow will be our doubts of today." — Franklin Delano Roosevelt

Success-Minded People are those who understand the principals of limits. There are times when limits serve us and those where they restrict us. Example: freedom does not mean that you can do anything you wish. Justice, honor and morality set limits on behavior. This is a good thing that keeps wicked and immoral people from doing great damage to the rest of society. Author Terry Prachett rightly said, *"Freedom without limits is just a word."* Or as writer Elbert Hubbard said, *"Responsibility is the price of freedom."*

There is also another side to limits, which is in the area of thinking, creating and dreaming. I think former President Ronald Reagan put it best when he said, *"There are no great limits to growth because there are no limits of human intelligence, imagination, and wonder."* When it comes to your God-given ability to dream and create, the only limits are those you set. English Philosopher Francis Bacon said, *"God has placed no limits to the exercise of the intellect He has given us on this side of the grave."*

Think about this: If there was no limit to what you could think up, what would you try to do? Removing the limits we have set on our imagination is like getting a free travel pass to anywhere in the world. It may be hard to grasp right now, but think about it, let the ideas flow and you will be amazed what you start to think about.

This causes me to think about Joshua in Scripture. In the first chapter of the book of Joshua, you see him in the promised land. Moses, who Joshua served for many years and was mentored by, is dead. What does God tell Joshua? *"Just as I have been with Moses, I will be with you; I will not fail you or forsake you."* (V: 5). Now think as if you were Joshua. You saw Moses do everything from parting the sea to getting water out of a rock. Now all that power is with you. No limits there. Think of what he must have felt.

God has that kind of freedom for you as well. Not a freedom from responsibility; but a freedom from limits. How have your self-imposed limits stopped you? Open the door, find new freedom and follow the path God has set for you. There is great power there. I think of what actor Vincent Price said, *"A man who limits his interests, limits his life."* **Success-Minded People** can live without limits. They can dream and do wonderful things.

"What the wicked fears will come upon him, and the desire of the righteous will be granted." – Proverbs 10:24

❖ ❖ ❖

Daily Thoughts: #43

HAVING THE RIGHT EQUIPMENT

"Each of us may be sure that if God sends us on stony paths, He will provide us with strong shoes, and He will not send us out on any journey for which He does not equip us well."
— Alexander MacLaren

One of the fears so many believers have is that God will call them to a task that they really do not want to do. They think that if they surrender their life fully to Christ, He will in turn call them to the deepest areas of Africa to suffer. That is not how God works. **Success-Minded People** find great comfort knowing that whatever the task God has called them to; He will equip them and give them the desire to do it.

This does not mean that every assignment from the Lord is happy and easy to do. In fact, He indeed has called some to suffer for Him. What it means is that we want nothing more than to do whatever He asks of us. The joy is in serving Him, not always in the task. As Pastor Michael Youssef said, *"Whenever God calls us to a task; He will equip us and enable us to complete that task."* His equipping is the key.

A mistake **Success-Minded People** can make is thinking that all service will end up in prosperity and comfort. Do not forget that for some, their God-given dream, their passion is the mission field. Their heart wants nothing more than to bring the Gospel of Christ to the lost all over the world. For some, that can mean suffering and difficulty. All the same it is their dream and worthy of all the effort that goes into any dream.

I have great respect for those who feel God has called them to a life in missions. This is a hard road yet one filled with great satisfaction. It takes a special person to do this work BUT God equips them for the task. Former broadcaster and author, John C. Broger said, *"The supreme challenge you will face in making Christ-honoring, biblical changes is dying to self. The biblical perspective concerning 'self' is exactly opposite to what the wisdom of this world proclaims."*

As a **Success-Minded Person**, I believe that for those of us who are not called to the mission field, we have a responsibility to support and equip those who are called. We are all commanded to bring the gospel of Christ to the entire world. If you do not go yourself, you must support those who go for you. Pastor and author T.D. Jakes said, *"The challenge of the believer is to take the faith that you got in here and take it to the place out there."*

"And He said to them, 'God into all the world and preach the gospel to all creation." — Mark 16:15

❖ ❖ ❖

Daily Thoughts: #44

LOVING YOUR JOB

"Find something you like to do so much that you'd gladly do it for nothing, and if you learn to do it well, someday people will be happy to pay you for it." – Unknown

D r. Charles Mayo, founder of the world famous Mayo Clinic made a wild statement when he said, *"There is no fun like work."* Really, this is the way it was meant to be. Somewhere we came up with the idea that work is bad and that we should do our best to do as little work as possible. Remember that work was around before the fall. Adam tended the garden before Eve, the apple or the serpent came into the picture. It only became labor after the fall.

The problem that many have is not that they hate work but they hate the work they do. **Success-Minded People** know that to find fulfillment in your job you need three elements, 1) something that plays to your strength set, 2) something that makes you feel like you are contributing to society, 3) something you love to do. When these elements are all present you have the closest thing to the "dream job."

Does this mean things become easy and there is no real work? The old saying, *"Find a job you love and you will never have to work again,"* is really not true. Fact is, when you are doing what you love to do, you work harder and longer. It is just that you have a joy in what you do. You feel that you are making things better and adding value to the world around you.

We, as human beings, were never created to be idle. You are made to work. Roman philosopher and poet Horace said, *"Life grants nothing to us mortals without hard work."* This idea that people have about not working or only doing the least they have to in order get by is so destructive to them and to our society as a whole. Hard work will not kill you, but laziness will make you wish that you were dead.

I hear so many excuses from people who are unemployed and not really looking for work, every excuse from the economy to not being ready for a job, (whatever that means). There are opportunities everywhere for you, not only to work, but to do the things you love. Thomas A. Edison said, *"Opportunity is missed by most people because it is dressed in overalls and looks like work."* You need to work. The longer you put it off, the more damage it will do to you.

Success-Minded People know that hard work is the price for success. If you do not pay the price, you will not enjoy the reward. Stop seeing work as something to avoid. Enjoy it, embrace it and you will find the satisfaction you are looking for in life.

"A man will be satisfied with good by the fruit of his words, and the deeds of a man's hands will return to him."
— Proverbs 12:14

❖ ❖ ❖

Daily Thoughts: #45

THE BEST CARD IN YOUR WALLET

"Books can take a person all over the world – a library card will take you father than a driver's license."
— Ruben Martinez

Success-Minded People know that there is no gift given them more powerful than the ability to read. Mark Twain said, *"The only thing sadder than a person who can't read is one who can but doesn't."* Reading is so key to your success in every area of life. One of the most tragic things I have read was a university study that said close to 40% of people who graduate from college never read a book again.

Through books you can travel to any place, learn any topic, explore other cultures, have a good laugh and be scared out of your wits. President Abraham Lincoln said, *"The things I want to know are in books; my best friend is the man who'll get me a book I ain't read."* Throughout history you will see that great leaders and people who made an impact on the world were readers. **Success-Minded People** find great power and encouragement between the covers of a book.

Please do not use the excuse that you get your knowledge from television, radio or CDs. All those things can be helpful, but they do not replace the importance of reading. I like what the great Groucho Marx said, *"I find television very educational. Every time somebody turns on the set, I go into the other room and read a book."*

Of course, the most important book you will ever read is the Bible. Its knowledge and wisdom is endless, and therefore you will never finish it. Bible reading should be a part of your daily routine. And it should be more than just a quick reading of a verse or two to say you did it. It needs to be studied and applied.

As a **Success-Minded Person** I encourage you to take the time to read, if you do not already. It can be fiction or non-fiction, whatever you like. I do encourage you to find books that line up with your goals and read with a purpose. The important thing is to read. You do not have to read fast, you do not have to read for hours on end. Start now and you will make it a habit you will enjoy.

Science fiction writer, Ray Bradbury said, *"There are some worse crimes than burning books. One of them is not reading them."* Do not neglect this tool that you have at your disposal. Nothing will bring you closer to a successful end than to read.

"Know that wisdom is thus for your soul; if you find it, then there will be a future, and your hope will not be cut off." — Proverbs 24:14

❖ ❖ ❖

Daily Thoughts: #46

YOU HAVE THE TIME

"There is never enough time to do everything, but there is always enough time to do the most important thing."
— Brian Tracy

One of the hottest topics around today is *time management*. If you go to Google and do a search on time management you will get 109,000,000 results. They cover classes, books, speakers, seminars and much more. Who has the time to look at all this stuff?

Success-Minded People know that time is a precious resource. You only get so much of it and as Benjamin Franklin said, *"Lost time is never found again."* Yet time is the great equalizer. No one on the planet has any more than the next guy. We all have only 24 hours in a day. The only difference is the number of days we get. It is not getting more time that is the answer; it is how we use our time.

Success-Minded People must look at time as something they can control. See that everything you do is planned, and done correctly. Coach John Wooden had it right when he said, *"If you don't have time to do it right, when will you have time to do it over?"* Properly using time for planning and learning will allow you more time to do other things. It is said that one hour of planning can save three hours of execution. You save a lot of time when you do not have to keep doing things over due to mistakes.

Israel's Former Prime Minister, Golda Meir said, *"I must govern the clock, not be governed by it."* A well-planned day can give you that power. This is also why being prepared for things is so important. The person who is ready for anything is a person who is not a victim of time. There is no last minute panic because something unexpected happened. To be prepared is to expect the unexpected.

The proper use of time really is not a complicated thing at all. **Success-Minded People** do not live by the seat of their pants. They look at a day, a project, an event or whatever they have coming and plan for it. They use their time wisely, and therefore they have time to use. There is no such thing as extra or more time, but there is the ability to free up some of the time you are allotted. A little planning goes a long way.

> *"Do this, knowing the time, that it is already the hour for you to awaken from sleep; for now salvation is nearer to us than when we believed."* — Romans 13:11

❧ ❧ ❧

Daily Thoughts: #47

BEING NEAR SIGHTED

"It is a terrible thing to see and have no vision."
— Helen Keller

When we talk about vision we usually are talking about looking to the future. We talk of dreams and goals and what will be when we have achieved our passions. But there is another type of vision that is as important, if not more, as looking ahead and that is the vision of looking at what is around you.

A problem many **Success-Minded People** have is to be so future-focused that we miss today. We see people and things as they seem in the moment and not by the potential they possess. It is the old *"not seeing the forest for the trees"* syndrome. Because of this we miss some of the things that would bring our goals closer. We also miss the potential that is in people that we could encourage, mentor and help along the way.

Let me give you an example. J. Oswald Sanders, author of the book Spiritual Leadership tells this story. *"The Pharisees looked at Peter and saw only an unschooled fisherman — not worth a second look. Jesus saw Peter as a prophet and preacher, saint and leader who helped turn the world upside down."* Was Peter different when he was with the Pharisees than he was when he was with Jesus? No, I do not believe he was. The difference was not in Peter; it was in the perspective of those who saw him.

Have you been with people and just seen what they appear to be? Have you see a man or woman who had little going for them, not much to offer and *"not worth a second look"*? Maybe you should look again with the vision of Jesus. You may see potential there that you never saw before. Remember, Peter was Peter. What Jesus saw was always there. He was created for this. The potential in others is always there, you just need to see it.

The person you overlook or see as nothing special may be the very person God will use to change everything. They may be the one to find a cure for cancer or to lead a nation to freedom. You never know what people are capable of until the moment God brings it out. **Success-Minded People** must always be on the lookout for those who have great potential. It is up to us to bring that to the surface and help them develop into the people God created them to be.

Before you get lost in the future, look around your present. See what God has placed before you now that you can help bring into fulfillment. You may be surprised what you will find.

"Therefore encourage one another and build up one another, just as you also are doing."   – 1 Thessalonians 5:11

❋ ❋ ❋

Daily Thoughts: #48

UNLOCKING LIFE'S TREASURES

"If love is the treasure, laughter is the key."
— Yakov Smirnoff

Okay. Here is a bit of instruction you will not get every day. At some point today, take some time to laugh. You heard right. Laugh till you cry. It will be one of the best and healthiest things you can do for yourself. There is nothing so refreshing than a good laugh. Comedian Milton Berle use to say, *"Laughter is an instant vacation."*

Did you know that a child will laugh over 300 times in a day? The average adult only laughs 15 times. What's up with that? It isn't that there is nothing to laugh at. The human race is the funniest thing going. I think that God must sit in heaven and laugh Himself silly looking at us. Just go to the mall sometime and sit and watch people. You will love it. And of course, laugh at yourself. The old proverb is, *"Blessed is he who can laugh at himself. He will never be without entertainment."*

Success-Minded People are people who like to laugh. That is why they do not live in depression or discouragement. You cannot be happy and sad at the same time. Humorist Mark Twain said, *"Against the assault of laughter* *nothing can stand."* Laughter is your weapon against the negative influences that are around you.

What do you do to get a good laugh? Here are a few ideas:

- Read the comics or books by humorists
- Watch funny movies
- Find a friend you like to laugh with and spend time together
- Play with some kids – learn from the experts on laughing

Charlie Chaplin said, *"A day without laughter is a day wasted."* I do not care what you do for work or how your life is going, take time and do a bit of laughing. Believe me you will feel better and you will do better. **Success-Minded People** know that a workplace where laughter and cheerfulness is encouraged is a more productive and better place to work. When people enjoy going to work and have fun with the people they work with, they are more productive and call off work less.

So your assignment for today is to laugh. Tell a joke, hear a joke, be a joke, whatever works for you. Have some fun and see if it does not change your day.

"A joyful heart makes a cheerful face, but when the heart is sad, the spirit is broken." – Proverbs 15:13

❖ ❖ ❖

Daily Thoughts: #49

LEARNING FROM CHILDREN

*"You have brains in your head. / You have feet in your shoes. /
You can steer yourself / Any direction you choose."*

— Dr. Seuss

How long has it been since you've played with a child? I'm not talking about babysitting or watching TV together. I mean really play with a child, entering into their world and allowing your adultness to drift away for a bit. Children take play very seriously. Fred Rogers (Mr. Rogers) tells us, *"Play is a child's work."* And if you spent any time playing you know how true that is.

Success-Minded People need to know that you can learn so much from a child. They can teach you the power of imagination and how simple true creativity is. As adults we struggle and strain to be creative and to think of new and better things. You will notice that a 6-year-old will recreate the world without breaking a sweat.

Children can show us that all things are possible. They can believe they can achieve anything from being president, a sports hero to walking on the moon. It is a paradox how we tell our children that they can be anything when they are small and that they need to be practical when they get older. Shouldn't we believe in the ability to achieve our dreams more when we are old enough to really do it?

Success-Minded People know that it is their responsibility to teach their children to be righteous, and good. Walt Disney said, *"Our heritage and ideas, our code and standards – the things we live by and teach our children are preserved or diminished by how freely we exchange ideas and feelings."*

A child will learn and remember more from the time they play with you than from all the schooling in the world. I am not against education, in fact, you know I am zealous about learning. But teaching our children the principals of life, their faith and standards to live by is not done in school. That is our responsibility, and we cannot neglect it. It can be achieved in two ways: 1) by example – you have to live it yourself for it to have power – and 2) by communication – you need to communicate on their level so they understand what you mean.

Albert Einstein said, *"The pursuit of truth and beauty is a sphere of activity in which we are permitted to remain children all our lives."* Spend time with children, play and enter their world of the possible. Slay a few dragons, save a princess or two and be a superhero for a day. You will be surprised on how it will change your outlook on things.

"Truly I say to you, unless you are converted and become like children, you will not enter the kingdom of heaven."
– Matthew 18:3

❧ ❧ ❧

Daily Thoughts: #50

REALLY BELIEVING

"The thing always happens that you really believe in; and the belief in a thing makes it happen."

– Frank Lloyd Wright

Success-Minded People must answer this question: *"What is your life going to be like?"* A simple positive confession answer of *"Great!"* will not do. You must know and believe in how you intend to live. This is not some ESP prediction of the future, it is belief. If you do not believe in your destiny, it will not happen. It is having faith that God will work in your life to help you fulfill your purpose. As economist Ben Stein put it, *"Faith is not believing that God can. It is knowing that God will."*

Success-Minded People are great at setting goals and working toward their dreams. Where they can fall short is when they face the obstacles that life always brings. It is at that time we start to wonder if we really will ever achieve our dream. Maybe we will do our best but fall just short of the goal? This kind of thinking slows us down and causes doubt and defeat. The **Success-Minded Person** must not allow this to happen.

Speaker and author of, <u>The Power of Positive Thinking</u>, Dr. Norman Vincent Peale said, *"Don't go crawling through life on your hands and knees half-defeated. Stand up to your obstacles and do something about them. You will find they haven't half the strength you think they have."* Always remember that the key to victory is action. Do not surrender to your problems, no matter how big they seem to be. Stand up and do something. Fight back. Take the victory that God has given you. Read Romans 8 and believe they you are more than a conqueror in Christ.

Success-Minded People must understand that the time for talk and debate is not when you are fighting for victory in life. Do you believe in your dream? Do you believe that you have a God-given purpose that is yours to fulfill? Scottish philosopher, Thomas Carlyle said, *"A man lives by believing something: not by debating and arguing about many things."* Do not allow the enemy of your soul to distract you or take your eyes off the prize.

Believe in God. Believe in yourself. Believe in your dream. Believe in your purpose. Believe that you can overcome any difficulty and problem because the God of the universe has made the way for you. If He is for us, who can be against us? You can do this, I know you can because I believe that God is able, and I believe in you.

"The hope of the righteous is gladness, but the expectation of the wicked perishes."   – Proverbs 10:28

❧ ❧ ❧

Daily Thoughts: #51

FACING FACTS

*"It's one thing to believe that you possess remarkable poten-
tial. It's another thing to have enough faith in yourself
that you think you can fulfill it."* – John C. Maxwell

Success-Minded People know that there is only one
certainty in life and that is truth. Despite what popular opinion my say, truth is not different for each of
us. It is never a matter of how you feel, think or desire to
believe. Truth is truth. It is the black and white of life. It is
not open to debate nor can it be changed. As former radio
personality Woodrow Kroll said, *"Truth can't be judged on the
basis of popularity."*

There are those who do not like to hear this kind of
talk. They are "offended" that someone would declare that
there is only one truth. Evangelist, David Jeremiah said,
*"Truth offends everyone outside its definitions. But the irony of
truth is that the greater its potential for offense, the greater its potential for giving hope."* There is great comfort in knowing that
there are some certainties in life.

Success-Minded People will always discuss the many
different areas of truth in life. There is spiritual truth, sci-
entific truth, and artistic truth and so on. None are a different truth, just truth about a different aspect of life. I want
you, however, to ponder the truth about you. Who are you,
and what you can achieve?

Author Darren L. Johnson said, *"Believing in who you are is a major part of a powerful combination for success."* If you believe that you are a **Success-Minded Person**, and I believe you are, you have to act like it. That is not a *"fake it till you make it"* type of thinking, it is a belief type thinking. If we believe something about ourselves, and we know it is true, we must then live in that truth.

Of course, just because you choose to believe something does not make it true. If I believed I were a great singer, it would not make me one (believe me I am not). Why not? Because the evidence shows that not to be true. I cannot sing and no matter how much I choose to believe, I will not be a singer. But I do know what gifts I do have, and I can accept that fact and live in my gifts. That is a fact, I know it is true, and it has proven itself to be true.

Success-Minded People understand that believing is not some mental shotgun blast where you believe in whatever it hits. Believing is based on facts, on knowledge and understanding. You know the facts, and you stand on them. There is always a reason for believing in something.

"...Do not be afraid any longer, only believe."
– Mark 5:36

❖ ❖ ❖

Daily Thoughts: #52

HALF TIME

"When you discover you've been leading only half a life, the other half is going to haunt you until you develop it."
— Phillips Brooks

Can a **Success-Minded Person** not be a Christian? That is a good question. I can say that there are many who are "successful" in their business or other endeavors and do not know Christ. However, I believe that to be truly successful one must have a complete life. There is not completeness in life without knowing Christ as your personal Lord and Savior.

Yes, that is a bold statement, but it was not me who made it. Jesus Himself said *"I am the way, the truth and the life. No one comes to the Father except by Me."* (John 14:6). How can you fully know who you are and what you were created to be unless you know the one who created you? For the **Success-Minded Person**, Christ is the center of your life. It is Him who we serve, Him from whom we find meaning and direction. Author Neil T. Anderson said, *"We don't serve God to gain His acceptance, we are accepted so we serve God. We don't follow Him in order to be loved; we are loved so we follow Him."*

"Yes" you may say, *"but can't you find God other than in Jesus?"* The answer is no. God sent His only Son to pay the price for your sin. We have all sinned and come short of God's standard, the Bible tells us. We need a Savior to pay the price for those sins. Jesus is the only one who has done

that. John Newton, author of the song Amazing Grace said, *"When I was young, I was sure of many things, now there are only two things of which I am sure: one is, that I am a miserable sinner, and the other, that Christ is an all-sufficient savior. He is well-taught who learns these two lessons."*

Success-Minded People must not allow the idea of success to cloud their minds from the real purpose of life. As stated in the Westminster Catechism: *"The chief aim of man is to love God and enjoy Him forever."* God loves you with a burning love. He has done everything for you to come into a relationship with Him through His Son Jesus Christ. All you have to do is believe and accept the salvation that is there for you.

Without Christ, there is no success in life. Scripture asks us, *"What profit is it if you gain the whole world and lose your own soul?"* **Success-Minded People** know that true success only comes to the life surrendered to Christ. In it there is real success, real happiness and real completion. As G.K. Chesterton said, *"The Christian ideal has not been tried and found wanting. It has been found difficult; and left untried."* May it not be so with you.

"For the Son of Man has come to seek and to save that which was lost."   – Luke 19:10

❖ ❖ ❖

Daily Thoughts: #53

PAYING THE PRICE

"It is easy to dodge our responsibilities, but we cannot dodge the consequences of dodging our responsibilities."
— Josiah Charles Stamp

We live in a very mixed up time. We demand more and more from our jobs, government, and family and yet seem to take less and less responsibility for ourselves. **Success-Minded People** can never expect greatness in life if they are unwilling to be responsible.

Responsibility for one's self means that you understand that there are no excuses in life. If you do not succeed; it is on you, not on the world. Mark Twain said it best, *"Don't go around saying the world owes you a living; the world owes you nothing, it was here first."* You cannot be a **Success-Minded Person** and expect to have others take care of you. It will not happen.

One of the things that a **Success-Minded Person** must do is to understand that all success has a price. If you are unwilling to pay the price you are not going to see the success. It is that simple. Nothing comes but through hard work and effort. Hard work is not a bad thing as some people would have you believe. There is nothing more fulfilling than to work hard at something and achieve success. That success is yours, you know that it is yours and you know you earned it. Tony Robbins said, *"Excuses are for the* *weak. Apathy for the lazy. Action for the motivated. Results for the determined. Success for the daring. "*

As a **Success-Minded Person** you must be willing to take the responsibility to bring your dreams into being. The first step is to take responsibility for yourself. Boy Scout founder, Robert Baden-Powell said, *"An individual step in character training is to put responsibility in the individual."* Understand the cost that is involved for you to succeed. Once you have taken that responsibility you are well on your way to success.

The late Napoleon Hill talked about the importance of writing down the amount you will pay for your chief aim in life. What will you give to achieve your success? If you do not figure it out and write it down, you will never know what you must do. You can only take responsibility for what you know. But when you do, and you determine in your heart to be responsible for it, you can do anything your heart desires. **Success-Minded People** are responsible people who understand self-respect and integrity. They can achieve when others just have excuses.

"Let integrity and uprightness preserve me, for I wait for you. "
                                                          – Psalm 25:21

❖ ❖ ❖

Daily Thoughts: #54

TIME FOR WORK

"Inaction breeds doubt and fear. Action breeds confidence and courage. If you want to conquer fear, do not sit at home and think about it. Go out and get busy."
– Dale Carnegie

I have told you several times that **Success-Minded People** understand the value of work. Nothing is achieved without action. It is a simple formula that I believe Zig Ziglar made clear when he said, *"It was character that got us out of bed, commitment that moved us into action, and discipline that enabled us to follow through."*

The trouble some people have is the actual step of taking action. They believe it is needed and that no success will be won without it; but there is a fear of the step itself. The fear could be of failure or that they will make a mistake. However, I believe that many **Success-Minded People** are not fearful they will fail but that they will succeed. Sounds odd? Not if you think about it.

Once you start action toward your goal, there is no turning back. **Success-Minded People** understand that by taking action they have begun the work. They have committed themselves to see that through, and therefore, cannot turn back. It is that fear, the fear of the journey actually beginning, that can stall them. It is like the soldier who prepares and dreams of war and then when faced with it finds himself trapped by fear. But they also know as W. Clement Stone said, *"Thinking will not overcome fear, but action will."*

It takes courage to get to work. It is not waiting until you know you can do it with no mistakes. British clergyman Cardinal Newman said, *"A man would do nothing, if he waited until he could do it so well that no one would find fault with what he has done."* To have courage is to take action. Courage does not stand still; it does not hide. Courage is not the absence of fear, but the ability to overcome fear and move forward.

What is holding you back from taking the action you need to? Management expert, Peter Drucker said, *"Plans are only good intentions unless they immediately degenerate into hard work."* Courage and action are qualities of **Success-Minded People**, so they are in you. Take the first step and get busy doing something. You will find that it is not as difficult as it seems. All boogie-men seem big and terrible in the dark; once you turn on the light, you see it is nothing but a shadow on the wall.

"Therefore we do not lose heart, but though our outer man is decaying, yet our inner man is being renewed day by day."　　　　　　　　　　　　– 2 Corinthians 4:16

❖ ❖ ❖

Daily Thoughts: #55

GOING ALL THE WAY

"When you believe in a thing, believe in it all the way, implicitly and unquestionably." — Walt Disney

One of the most common tragedies in life is the great number of people who pursued their dream and gave up just before they could have achieved it. Many were just one step away or one more try. But they were not willing to go all the way. As Thomas A. Edison said, *"Many of life's failures are people who did not realize how close they were to success when they gave up."*

The operative words in that quote are, *"they gave up"*. **Success-Minded People** see that to give up is an action just as moving forward is. It takes a decision, and you must act. People who give up will never succeed. They will be a victim to the challenges of life at every turn, and they will fold under those challenges. **Success-Minded People** do not give up.

Study after study show that the difference between those who achieve their goals in life and those that do not is that those who achieve do not quit. Success expert, Peter Lowe said, *"The most common trait I have found in all successful people is that they have conquered the temptation to give up."* This does not mean that it was easy for a successful person. They had to work hard, harder than those who quit, because they stayed with it.

The great coach Vince Lombardi said, *"The difference between a successful person and others is not a lack of strength, not a lack of knowledge, but rather a lack of determination."* This is why it is such a tragedy; those who quit had all that the one who succeeded did, but chose not to use it.

Success-Minded People know that the road ahead will be rough. We do not know how long it will take to achieve our dream. The truth is, it does not matter how long. Our determination is not on process but on the goal. There is no question, we will succeed. We know as Winston Churchill said, *"Continuous effort – not strength or intelligence – is the key to unlocking our potential."*

As a **Success-Minded Person**, do not think about giving up. Your victory is coming. The goal you desire is achievable if you do not stop. When will you win? When you have achieved what you are striving for, not a moment before. The only way you can lose is to give up and you will not do that – so – you will not lose.

"You, however, continue in the things you have learned and became convinced of, knowing from whom you have learned them." — 2 Timothy 3:14

❧ ❧ ❧

Daily Thoughts: #56

USING YOUR GIFTS

"All Christians are called to develop God-given talents, to make the most of their lives, to develop to the fullest their God-given powers and capacities." – J. Oswald Sanders

As a **Success-Minded Christian**, a believer in Jesus Christ, you have a responsibility to change the world. That sounds like an awfully big order doesn't it? But that is what we are told to do. We are salt and light. We are to be the example to the rest of the world. The Church of Jesus Christ (that is us if you don't know) is commanded to bring the gospel to every nation.

God has given each and every one of us gifts and talents that we are to use for His purposes. That does not mean that we all have to go into ministry, but we are all to be part of His great plan. A.B. Simpson, founder of the Christian Missionary Alliance church said, *"God means every Christian to be effective, to make a difference in the actual records and results of Christian work. God puts each of us here to be a power. There is not one of us who is not an essential wheel of the machinery and can accomplish that which God calls us to do."*

Success-Minded People need to be aware that they are an example all the time to those who are in the world. In business and in our personal life, people are watching to see what we do and how we live. That is why it is so important that you do not allow yourself to slide into indifference and the life style of the world. Leonard Ravenhill put it best when he said, *"How can you pull down the strongholds of Satan if you don't have the strength to turn off your TV?"*

For **Success-Minded People** there is no difference between the spiritual and the secular. They are not one way when they are being spiritual and another when with non-Christian friends. We are who we are all the time. Former Congressman, J.C. Watts said, *"Character is doing the right thing when nobody's looking. There are too many people who think that the only thing that's right is to get by, and the only thing that's wrong is to get caught."* That is not the case for the **Success-Minded Person**. We know that we must live rightly all the time. It is who we are.

Use the gifts God has given you. Be successful in all you do. It is the life of **Success-Minded People** that will show the world that the ways of the Lord are good and bring life. They are not restrictive and burdensome. God has a plan, a good plan, and we are all part of that plan. Be the best you can be and bring glory to God by your example to the world.

"Commit your works to the Lord, and your plans will be established."   – Proverbs 16:3

❖ ❖ ❖

Daily Thoughts: #57

WINNING

"If winning isn't everything, why do they keep score?"
— Vince Lombardi

Who ever came up with the idea that no one is supposed to win in a game? We teach children that we are all winners, and there are no losers. That is bunk and totally untrue. We may think that we are saving our children from being hurt, but what we are doing is setting them up to fail in life. That is wrong, and right from the pit of hell.

Life is full of winning and losing. When we teach people that they cannot lose we teach them that they cannot win either. If all are equal, why try to do better? Why should someone put forth the effort to succeed if they are only as good as the next guy? There is no advantage and no motivation in life. This is why we have so many who live hopeless lives thinking that everyone else should take care of them.

Success-Minded People know that there is a win and lose in life. As in sports, the better you are, the more games you win. It takes skill and preparation to win in life. George Allen said, *"Winning is the science of being prepared."* You must take what you have and make it into the best talent it can be. John Maxwell points out in his book, <u>Talent is Never Enough</u>, that we are all created with equal value, but we are not equally gifted. Some have greater talents than others; but we all have talents we can use.

Success-Minded People know that sometimes you will win and sometimes you will lose. Losing is not bad if you can learn and improve by it. Real estate investor Donald Trump said, *"Sometimes by losing a battle you find a new way to win the war."* That is right thinking. You do not have to be protected from losing; you just have to learn from it.

Please understand that there is no fair in life. We were not all given an equal playing field. Some people can perform better than others. That does not mean they have more value than others. We all have value and we all have a purpose, but we will not be given equal victories in life. You have to win those. You have to do your best to be your best. You have to take action to win. **Success-Minded People** are winners because they take action and do all they can to achieve, while others wait for someone to just give them a life.

"But in all these things we overwhelmingly conquer through Him who loved us."   – Romans 8:37

❖ ❖ ❖

Daily Thoughts: #58

LAUGHING AT HEROES

"We make men without chests and expect of them virtue and enterprise. We laugh at honor and are shocked to find traitors in our mist." — C.S. Lewis

When I have told people of my love for the Boy Scouts and belief that the Scout Law is a foundation for right living, I get looks like I am a bit off. People, good people, think that the Scout Law is a bit outdated and impractical. I find that very sad.

Success-Minded People need to understand that the principles that make us a civil and righteous people are the same now as they always were. To think things like trustworthiness, loyalty, helpfulness, kindness are old fashioned is to believe the Ten Commandments are outdated (some believe that too). As Dr. Martin Luther King, Jr. said, *"The time is always right to do what is right."*

Too many of us have become complacent and fuss and whine about the state of our society. The answer is not to complain about it but to start changing it. President Ronald Reagan said, *"To sit back hoping that someday, some way, someone will make things right is to go on feeding the crocodile, hoping he will eat you last – but eat you he will."* If things are going to change, they must start with you.

The qualities of **Success-Minded People** are those very qualities listed in the Scout Law. It is never outdated to do what is right, to care for others and to be an honorable and loyal person. We must teach it to our children and to those with whom we come in contact. It is more than just not doing wrong, it is doing right. *"Discernment"* said Charles Spurgeon *"is not a matter of simply telling the difference between right and wrong; rather it is telling the difference between right and almost right."*

Success-Minded People can change the world if they will only be willing to change themselves and live as an example to those around them. Being a hero is not a corny thing that you should fear. We have the power to recapture our society and change things for the good. The only reason things went downhill was that good people no longer fought for what was right. We resigned to the thinking of others who told us we were no longer relevant. It's time to stand and say there is a right and a wrong. We believe in what is right, and that is the most relevant thing there is.

"Put on the full armor of God, so that you may be able to stand firm against the schemes of the devil."

– Ephesians 6:11

❖ ❖ ❖

Daily Thoughts: #59

IT IS ALL CONNECTED

"If you can dream it, then you can achieve it."

— Zig Ziglar

You can tell a lot about a person by their dreams. **Success-Minded People** who are excited about life and are determined to become more than what they are, have clear, well defined dreams. You can ask them and they will tell you – in detail – where they are going in life and how they will get there. People of low ambition who achieve little in life, have no idea what their dreams are or live in fantasies of winning lotteries and easy money. American philosopher and author, Henry David Thoreau said, *"Dreams are the touchstones of our character."*

Success-Minded People take the first step to realizing their dreams by taking responsibility for them. Irish poet, William Butler Yeats said, *"In dreams begin responsibility."* **Success-Minded People** know that if their dreams are to become reality, it is up to them to make it happen. No one will do it for them, not even God. The Lord expects us to be responsible and to follow the directions He has given us. Les Brown said, *"If you take responsibility for yourself, you will develop a hunger to accomplish your dreams."*

A dream without the action to achieve is nothing but wishful thinking. It is like smoke, you can see it in the room but you cannot grab it and hold onto it. Responsibility means action. It means that you have a plan for the achievement of your dreams, and you will take whatever steps you must to achieve it. No excuses, no blaming others for your shortcomings. You stand as Hannibal did facing the mountains and say, "We will find a way or make one."

Success-Minded People also dream big dreams. Small dreams that are easily achieved are no challenge for the person of success. German philosopher von Goethe said, *"Dream no small dreams for they have no power to move the hearts of men."* Dreams must have power. They must be big enough for you to know that they are impossible. Once we believe in the impossible, we are able to achieve it. Sounds off, I know, but think about it. Everything we have and do in our world was once believed to be impossible.

The key to achieving all dreams is to take action and make it happen. **Success-Minded People** must take the words of 17th century thinker, Baltasr Gracian to heart when he said, *"Dreams will get you nowhere, a good kick in the pants will take you a long way."* Believe in your impossible dream and take responsibility for it. When you do, you will achieve it and far more. Dreams do not end; they only give birth to greater dreams along the way.

> *"For the vision is yet for the appointed time; it hastens toward the goal and it will not fail. Though it tarries, wait for it, for it will certainly come, it will not delay."*
> – Habakkuk 2:3

❖ ❖ ❖

Daily Thoughts: #60

YOUR COMING ATTRACTIONS

"Imagination is everything. It is the preview of life's coming attractions." — Albert Einstein

Can you imagine what it would be like to fly, to see the world from the viewpoint of a bird gliding on the wind? Imagine how it would feel to soar over fields, look at the tops of mountains and go from one place to another without having to stop for traffic or other obstacles. If you can imagine that, you have a slight peek into the minds of Orville and Wilbur Wright.

Understand that back in the early 1900s the idea of flight was impossible and only a crazy dreamer would dare to think of such a thing. But as writer Orison Swett Marden said, *"All men who have achieved great things have been great dreamers."* The Wright Brothers had a dream, and they could imagine a future where men could fly in a heavier-than-air machine. They saw the future, and it belonged to them.

This has been true for every invention that has changed the lives of humankind. From the printing press to the computer, people with imagination saw what others did not see — the future. American preacher Henry Ward Beecher said, *"The soul without imagination is what an observatory would be without a telescope. "* Imagination is one of the greatest and most wondrous gifts God has given to us.

Success-Minded People know that their imagination is a tool by which they can not only see the future, but create it. They understand that there is nothing that can hold back the creative mind from imagining wonders yet to be seen. **Success-Minded People** do not believe as Charles H. Duell, Commissioner of the U.S. Patent Office in 1899 did when he said, *"Everything that can be invented has been invented."* **Success-Minded People** know that we have only begun.

We have talked many times of all that we can learn from children; imagination is one of the best lessons. Children believe that anything is possible. They can imagine things far beyond our reasoning. Do not lose that power in yourself. Children can do little with their dreams while they are children. We as adults can make them all come true if we do not lose sight of them. Mark Twain said, *"You can't depend on your eyes when your imagination is out of focus."*

What is the wonder that God has placed in your heart? What impossible thing is rolling around in you that is struggling to get out? You can take us places we never dreamed we could go.

"...It's God's Spirit in a person, the breath of the Almighty One, that makes wise human insight possible." – Job 32:8

❖ ❖ ❖

Daily Thoughts: #61

YOUR PAST IS NOT YOUR FUTURE

"Make yourself an honest man, and then you may be sure there is one less rascal in the world." – Thomas Carlyle

During political campaigns you hear all kinds of things about the candidates and their past personal lives. Have you ever thought, *"I would never run for office because they would have a field day with my past."* I have. I have not hidden my past from people. I was a 60's child by all definitions of the word. I have much in my past that I am ashamed of and wish I had not done. I believe most **Success-Minded People** can say the same thing. We were not born with a success mind set, we grew into it.

I also know that back in 1974 I gave my life to Jesus Christ and all the past was forgiven. I was redeemed by His blood that He shed for me. That did not make my past go away, but I am no longer burdened by it. What **Success-Minded People** must understand is that none of us are perfect. We all made mistakes in life, and some of them were big mistakes. But our past does not equal our future.

Evil people will always use our past to make us back down on what is right. They call Christians hypocrites because we preach righteousness and have had sin in our own past. But that is the point. We know what is wrong and what is right and have chosen what is right. The fact that

I was once a fool does not mean that right is any less right. Alistair Begg said, *"Just because someone is sincere in his convictions does not mean that it is true. It is possible to be sincerely wrong."* It is the Bible that gives us the standard for life, not what we do or believe.

Success-Minded People cannot be bullied by evil men and women because of their past. We have done wrong and we have admitted so. Now we can stand for what is right. When one of the Union generals told President Lincoln that God was on their side, Lincoln replied, *"Sir, my concern is not whether God is on our side. My greatest concern is to be on God's side, for God is always right."* So it is with us. It is we who have come to God's side of things. He is right, not us.

The Presbyterian leader, A.A. Hodge said, *"It is easy to find a score of men wise enough to discover the truth than to find one intrepid enough, in the face of opposition, to stand up for it."* Be that one who will stand and say you believe in truth and righteousness. Be the **Success-Minded Person** who will let their past die and presently live for God. Stand for what is right, and no one will be able to stand against you.

"Do not be wise in your own eyes; fear the Lord and turn away from evil."   – Proverbs 3:7

❖ ❖ ❖

Daily Thoughts: #62

WHERE ARE YOU LOOKING?

"If you look up, there are no limits." – Japanese Proverb

Success-Minded People know that attitude is everything. Having said that, I also know that people treat a positive attitude like they do the idea of faith. They say they believe it, and they can quote it to you and tell you all the ways to use it, but in real life they tend to ignore it. Highly successful businessman and author W. Clement Stone said, *"There is little difference in people, but that little difference makes a big difference. The little difference is attitude. The big difference is whether it is positive or negative."*

Success-Minded People with a positive attitude just flat out do better than people who are negative. Positive people enjoy life more, succeed at more things and have more friends. As Zig Ziglar simply put it, *"Positive thinking will let you do everything better than negative thinking will."* The choice is always up to you. No one can create or destroy your attitude. You can strengthen it or surrender it, but no one can take it from you.

Success-Minded People know that they must work on their attitude all the time. It is affected by the things they read, listen to and see. They control it by their posture and thoughts. The Traveler's Gift author, Andy Andrews, said, *"My life – my personality, my habits, even my speech – is a combination of the books I choose to read, the people I choose to listen to, and the thoughts I choose to tolerate in my mind."*

If you have ever had the pleasure to listen to Mr. Andrews speak, you will see that whatever he does is working. He is a delight.

Where is your focus? Are you looking up and seeing no limits or down and seeing the ground? Look up and enjoy the freedom you have to become whatever you desire. Dreams are always visible in the sky, not in the muck. I love what Charles Lindbergh said after his historic flight across the Pacific: *"It is the greatest shot of adrenaline to be doing what you wanted to do so badly. You almost feel like you could fly without the plane."*

Don't dismiss the idea of a positive attitude as just *"success talk."* You attitude will determine where you end up in life. **Success-Minded People** know that there is no place for a negative and sour attitude. It only leads to destruction. But those who maintain a positive state of mind can achieve more than they ever thought possible. And their possible is already pretty big.

"Bright eyes gladden the heart; good news puts fat on the bones."
                                                        – Proverbs 15:30

❈ ❈ ❈

Daily Thoughts: #63

SMARTER BY THE MINUTE

"Attitudes are more important than intelligence."
— David J. Schwartz

We just talked of the importance of a positive attitude; now let's talk about the reality of a positive attitude. By reality, I mean what a good positive attitude really is. **Success-Minded People** know that being positive is not a refusal to see any negative or bad in the world. Positive people are very aware that bad things happen, bad people exist and there will always be pain and suffering somewhere in the world. As holocaust survivor, Corrie ten Boom said, *"The first step on the way to victory is to recognize the enemy."*

So how can **Success-Minded People** keep positive through all this? By training themselves to see that attitude is a choice and that, no matter what happens, there is a positive affect that can be gained. As Brian Tracy said, *"Winners make it a habit of manufacturing their own positive expectations in advance of the event."* The decision to be positive has been made; now they just maintain that attitude.

Success-Minded People have another advantage to keeping positive. They have broad interests and get involved in many different things. People who are negative seem not to get involved with anything and their interests are very few. Actor Vincent Price said, *"A man who limits his interest, limits his life."* There is so much wonder in the world about which you cannot help but feel positive and hopeful. Even in the mist of hard times you know that you will make it through. It is not that you might make it through, but that you *will* make it through, and with a high hand.

Success-Minded People also prepare to be positive. It is a deliberate act on their part. Some think that positive people are just that way, and they can't help it. The truth is that, left on our own, we will drift towards negative, not positive. Act like a dead fish, and you will always float down stream. Act like a live fish, filled with fight, and you will scale waterfalls. Former Yale University President, William Graham Summer said, *"What we prepare for is what we shall get."* If you are ready to be positive and win in life, you will achieve it.

As a **Success-Minded Person** you must understand that being positive is not the denial of the negative, but the denial of being conquered by it. Most people who fail in life were not beaten in battle but rather just laid down and allowed life to run over them. How sad that is. You have the God of the universe behind you to stand with you and guide you. How can you fail? How can anyone over-take you? Scripture tells us that *"if God is for us who can be against us?"*

> *"A man has joy in an apt answer, and how delightful is a timely word."*　　　　　　　　　　　　　　　– Proverbs 15:23

❖ ❖ ❖

Daily Thoughts: #64

BEING A WISE GUY

"A wise man will make more opportunities than he finds."
— Francis Bacon

We often think of a wise person as being someone who is intelligent, well-schooled and accomplished. **Success-Minded People** know that is not the case. We have all known some very well-educated fools and successful people who destroy themselves with foolish behavior. Wisdom is common sense along with doing what is right. Author J. Oswald Sanders said, *"If knowledge is the accumulation of facts, and intelligence the development of reason, wisdom is heavenly discernment. It is insight into the heart of things."*

A wise person knows that there is a right way and a wrong way to live. They will not give into the fads or reasoning of others but will stand for truth and what is right. They know that negative behavior will lead to a negative life. Greek poet Euripides said, *"Cleverness is not wisdom."* Many people think that they are wise because they can figure out how to get around doing what is right. Bad behavior is always a mark of foolishness.

Wisdom requires thinking. You must know what is best for others, as well as yourself. This is what is called common sense, which by the way is not that common anymore. We live in a time when people are encouraged to think of themselves first. We are encouraged to do what is best for us, at all cost. Even **Success-Minded People** can be convinced that in order to succeed, they can do "*whatever it takes.*" Even if you have to bend the rules or be a bit shady, the end always justifies the means. That is foolishness of the highest degree.

Success-Minded People must understand that there is a standard that we must hold for ourselves that is higher than that for others. Yes, you must do what is needed to succeed, but that never – **ever** – means compromising your integrity and values. Nineteenth Century American Theologian Albert Barnes stated: "*There is nothing more foolish than an act of wickedness; there is no wisdom equal to that of obeying God.*"

Be a wise person, and do what is right. Live by the high standards of **Success-Minded People,** and be the example we are to be to the world. When people know that you will not compromise, even for your own advancement, they will trust and respect you. Fools will fear you. Nothing is more threatening to those who behave foolishly than the light of those who do what is right. All sin and bad behavior is done in the dark, and as we are told in Scripture, the darkness hates the light. The **Success-Minded Person** lives in the light.

"*Let no one look down on your youthfulness, but rather in speech, conduct, love, faith and purity, show yourself an example of those who believe.*"   – 1 Timothy 4:12

❖ ❖ ❖

Daily Thoughts: #65

LEAVING YOUR MARK

"You can't leave footprints in the sands of time if you're sitting on your butt. And who wants to leave butt prints in the sands of time?" — Bob Moawad

There is an old saying that goes, *"You cannot plough a field by turning it over in your mind."* **Success-Minded People** understand that by only dreaming or wishing they could change things, will not make it happen. There must always be action and that action must come from us. Irish author Sean O'Casey said, *"Every action in our lives touches on some cord that will vibrate in eternity."* What you do matters.

Success-Minded People know that what they do will affect generations to come. They have the ability to put their mark, good or bad, on those who come after them. Self-focused people think only about their gain and how their actions will benefit them – that *"what is in it for me"* thinking that marks a selfish person. But the **Success-Minded Person** thinks in terms of how their action will affect those who follow how they will leave their mark on the world to come. Rugby player, Nelson Henderson said, *"The true meaning of life is to plant trees, under whose shade you do not expect to sit."*

Ask yourself, *"What am I doing that will outlive me?"* This is not measured in money or material things. I am not talking of leaving a fortune to your children. It is the values and the lessons you leave that count. What is better, to leave wealth to your children so they never have to achieve on their own, or to leave them the lessons and principles that teach them to build their own wealth? Pastor and author Rick Warren said, *"Love leaves legacy. How you treat other people, not your wealth or accomplishments, is the most enduring impact you can leave on earth."*

As a **Success-Minded Person**, I encourage you to take action, make your dreams come true, but do it with purpose. See all success as something that outlives a moment in time. Make yourself, those around you and the world better. This quote of Ralph Waldo Emerson marks my life as a personal standard to follow.: *"To laugh often and much; to win the respect of intelligent people and the affection of children; to earn the appreciation of honest critics and endure the betrayal of false friends; to appreciate beauty, to find the best in others; to leave the world a bit better, whether by a healthy child, a garden patch or a redeemed social condition; to know even one life has breathed easier because you have lived. This is to have succeeded."*

"Come, you children, listen to me; I will teach you the fear of the Lord."   – Psalm 34:11

❖ ❖ ❖

Daily Thoughts: #66

SETTING THE FUTURE

"Your current situation does not determine your future. Your future is determined by your decisions to succeed."

— Tony Robbins

Decisions always seem like a stumbling block to so many people. We all desire to make good and wise decisions but are not sure of our self enough to just step out. Some want to get as much information as they can before making a decision, and some just fear making a bad decision. The problem comes down to the fact that a decision is not being made. The late Jim Rohn said, *"It doesn't matter which side of the fence you get off on sometimes. What matters most is getting off. You cannot make progress without making decisions."*

It is true that some people are good decision makers by nature. For them it is not a big issue. But for most of us it can be the biggest distraction to our progress that we face. **Success-Minded People** need to understand this simple fact about decision making. Studies show that the best decision makers make decisions quickly and change them slowly, and poor decision makers make decisions slowly and change them quickly.

Forget your past. The past does not equal the future. **Success-Minded People** are always looking for ways to grow and become better. In the area of decision making, you need to start making decisions and trust your guts as to what it should be. Pastor and author, Robert H. Schuller said, *"High achievers spot rich opportunities swiftly, make big decisions quickly and move into action immediately. Follow these principles, and you can make your dreams come true."*

Success-Minded People do not wait for their future to happen. They make it happen. They know that the decisions they make will make them. Therefore, **Success-Minded People** work hard to maintain those decisions daily. John C. Maxwell said, *"Successful people make right decisions early, and manage those decisions daily."* You do not have to make the same decision over and over again. You make the decision once, and then you maintain it daily.

Indecision is the same as inaction. It gets you nowhere. It is like the old Chinese proverb that says *"He who deliberates fully before taking a step will spend his entire life on one leg."* **Success-Minded People** learn from all their own experiences, as well as those they observe in others. That way they can use that knowledge to make good, wise decisions in the future.

"Let us choose for ourselves what is right; let us know among ourselves what is good."   − Job 34:4

❖ ❖ ❖

Daily Thoughts: #67

STRONGER THAN A TREE

"If you don't like how things are, change it! You're not a tree." — Jim Rohn

I s there anything more draining than listening to a person who fusses and complains about their life all the time? They don't like their job, their friends, their bills are too high and income too low. What you want to say to them – in the most loving way of course – is, *"If you don't like your life, why don't you change it?"* Basketball great Michael Jordan had it right when he said, *"Some people want it to happen, and some wish it would happen, others make it happen."*

Success-Minded People have heard all the excuses, and have used a few themselves, for why people do not change their lives. The fact is, you are the only person who can change it. The problem is that too many people do not want to change. Change takes work, and besides, what will they complain about? Author Larry Randolph said, *"Practically speaking, the difference between success and failure for many will be determined by a willingness to accommodate change."*

Success-Minded People know that changing our life is not something that happens overnight. It is a process that takes time, but change is possible for those who are willing to do it. Author Seth Godin rightly said, *"You don't win an Olympic gold medal with a few weeks of intensive training. There's no such thing as an overnight sensation."* For change to happen, it must be deliberate and constant. On and off thoughts of change will not cut it.

Start with small changes first, things that you can do right now. Then as you begin to see the change taking affect, start to handle the details and build everyday on what you have started. Coach John Wooden said, *"It's the little details that are vital. Little things make big things happen."* The key to it all is to recognize that you must make them happen; it will not happen on its own. Former President John F. Kennedy said, *"Things do not happen. They are made to happen."*

Success-Minded People have no place to complain about their life. As Jim Rohn said in the opening quote, you can change it, *"you're not a tree"*. You are not stuck with the things in your life that bring you down. You have the power to change it or to change your attitude about it. Either way you will become the **Success-Minded Person** you were born to be.

"Therefore if anyone is in Christ, he is a new creature; the old things passed away; behold, new things have come."
— 2 Corinthians 5:17

❖ ❖ ❖

Daily Thoughts: #68

GREATER POWER

"Never underestimate your power to change yourself."
– H. Jackson Brown, Jr.

We talked about the need for change; now let's look at the reason why. **Success-Minded People** do not change just for something to do. Change is never good when it is just for the sake of change. That is why you need to know what to change and what that change will bring. Hallis Vaughn said, *"A ship's rudder gives direction while the vessel is in motion, not while it sits in the port."* You have to have a reason for change for change to work.

Success-Minded People have often experienced the feeling that something is not right, you need to make a change in your life. But change to what? Well, I think the more important question is, why do you need to change? If you did change, what would your life be like? By looking at the results you expect, you can start to figure out why you need the change. Are you unhappy? Well just changing will not make you happy. What are you doing that makes you unhappy? What behavior do you need to start or stop to move you in the right direction?

Ralph Waldo Emerson said, *"Once you make a decision, the universe conspires to make it happen."* Once you know what the problem or obstacle is, and you can identify it, you have won half the battle. This is why so many people are always looking for something to change them. It could be religion, success, education, marriage or anything. They hope that once they "do" something, they will change. What they do not know is why they have to change. You cannot get results if you do not know what you are expecting. It is like traveling. How do you know when you arrive if you do not know where you are going?

Success-Minded People know that they have standards to follow in life. First, there is God's standard and then that of a **Success-Minded Person**. These allow us to measure where we are at in life and where we need to be. Your fulfillment in life will never be away from God's standard. Author Larry Randolph said, *"In all of its glory, yesterday is still yesterday and can never replace the need for God's presence today."* The most natural and most powerful longing in the human heart is to have a relationship with God.

Seek out what God wants in your life. You can find it in two key ways: reading the Bible and prayer. Make that a habit in your daily life, and you will see change happen that you did not know you needed. Allow the Holy Spirit to transform you, and you will know what needs to change and why. And best of all, you will have the power behind you to make that change.

"He who gets wisdom loves his own soul; he who cherishes understanding prospers." — Proverbs 19:8

❖ ❖ ❖

Daily Thoughts: #69

BEYOND OUR DREAMS

"We all have possibilities we don't know about. We can do things we don't even dream we can do." – Dale Carnegie

Success-Minded People know that all things are possible to them – but at a cost. That's right, at a cost. Just because you know that you have it in you to achieve far beyond your dreams doesn't mean you will do so. Most people do not reach their potential simply because they are not willing to do what is needed to get there. What is needed? In a word: Discipline. And in the words of Coach Pat Riley, *"Discipline is not a nasty word."*

Success-Minded People achieve because they understand that the exercise of self-discipline and self-control is a must. If you cannot control your passions and habits, they will take you down every time. Jerry Bridges, author of <u>The Pursuit of Holiness</u>, wrote: *"Self-control is the exercise of inner strength under the direction of sound judgment that enables us to do, think, and say the things that are pleasing to God."* True potential is not an absence of restraint, but the ability to control those things that hold us back.

So what are the elements that keep us from discovering our true potential? Things like anger, resentment, selfishness, greed, sensual passions, and addictive habits. All of these are killers to your growth and ability as a **Success-Minded Person**. All must be controlled…by you. Nineteenth Century poet Sir Alfred Lord Tennyson said,

"The happiness of a man in this life does not consist in the absence but in the mastery of his passions." Get that? The *mastery* of your passions.

It is a simple truth that you will either master your passions, or they will master you. One of you will be the master, and the other will be the slave. As Charles C. Nobel said, *"First we make our habits, then our habits make us."* Self-control is nothing more than a habit. Discipline is doing the same thing, the right way every time. You cannot achieve greatness in any area of life without it. Pastor Roy L. Smith said it so clearly when he said, *"Discipline is the refining fire by which talent becomes ability."*

Do not allow bad habits, lack of self-control and a want for discipline to keep you from what God has for you. If you can control your passions, you will unleash power unlike you ever imagined. Look at the lives of truly great achievers, and you will see that self-control is the foundation of all greatness. Let nothing, not even you, hold you back.

"You are from God, little children, and have overcome them; because greater is He who is in you than he who is in the world."
                                                      – 1 John 4:4

❖ ❖ ❖

Daily Thoughts: #70

A BRAND NEW FINISH

"Though no man can go back and make a brand new start, anyone can start from now and make a brand new ending." – Carl Bard

One of the things we evangelicals like to claim is that coming to Jesus allows us to start life over, fresh and new. While I understand what is meant by that, I must say it is only partly true. You see, through Christ we receive forgiveness of sins and we do begin a new life in Him. But the old does not disappear. I wish I could say it did. But the truth is that the past is the past, and nothing changes it. We may no longer be captive to it, or under the burden of the past, but we cannot undo what was done.

That may seem distressing to some, but I see it as a very positive thing. You see you are allowed to start from where you are and make a new ending. It doesn't matter what you have done, the mistakes you have made, because you can still finish on top. Forgiveness is not the denial of the past; it is payment for the past. Your sins and brokenness was bought by Christ on the Cross. Your past is not erased, but it does not belong to you anymore.

Success-Minded People know that although they have failed in the past, and may well fail at times in the future, their ending still can be great and full of promise. Winston Churchill said, *"Success consists of going from failure to failure without loss of enthusiasm."* It is amazing how well you can do when you know you cannot fail, when you know that you will make it and achieve your dreams. You know that even if you hit a bump or two in the road, it will not knock you off course. There is an old Japanese proverb that says, *"Fall seven times, stand up eight."*

Success-Minded People have the courage to face their todays because they know they are not bound by their yesterdays. Our past kept telling us we could not make things right, and therefore, we cannot move forward. Christ tells us that He paid for the past, and we are now free to go forward with no fear of failing. This does not mean that it is smooth sailing from now on. Your toughest battles are yet to come. It does mean that you can face them knowing you have a new and better future before you. C.S. Lewis said, *"You are never too old to set another goal or to dream a new dream."*

Chinese Christian leader Watchman Nee said, *"The Christian experience, from start to finish, is a journey of faith."* And so it is. Start your journey now. Leave the past behind, and start a new ending.

> *"As far as the east is from the west, so far has He removed our transgressions from us."* – Psalm 103:12

❖ ❖ ❖

Daily Thoughts: #71

OFF BALANCE

"The past does not equal the future."   – Tony Robbins

Success-Minded People know not to look in the rear-view mirror of life to move forward. People too often look at the coming battles with the remembrance of past failures. What happened yesterday does not dictate what is to happen today. In the words of Queen Elizabeth I of England, *"The past cannot be cured."* Having said that, I will again add that it is what we do today that matters. Dr. John C. Maxwell said, *"Successful people conquer their feelings and form the habits of doing things unsuccessful people do not like to do."*

The exciting thing for **Success-Minded People** when they look forward is that they know the future is not formed yet. We have the power to change it because we have the power to change ourselves. Management expert, Peter Drucker said, *"The best way to predict the future is to create it."* When you are a **Success-Minded Person** you have decided what your main goal in life is. You are certain of your purpose and what you plan to achieve in life. Yes, you may not know the details of the journey yet, but that is not as important as knowing the destination.

Former U.S. President Abraham Lincoln stated, *"The best thing about the future is that it comes one day at a time."* You do not have to know every detail of what will happen or how your day will go in order to be sure of where you will end up. You will have battles along the way, make some detours and adjustments, but the **Success-Minded Person** sees the prize ahead and keeps moving in that direction.

The greatest tool you have to move you forward, leaving the past behind, is the power of your dream. This is why it is so important for you to write it down in as much clear detail as you can. Dreams fuel our engine and move us through the impossible. As former First Lady Eleanor Roosevelt said, *"The future belongs to those who believe in the beauty of their dreams."* **Success-Minded People** believe fully in their dreams.

Become a **Success-Minded Person** who is going into the future full of confidence and certainty. Know that you can change from what you were to who you are. Consultant Laddie F. Huter said, *"Success consists of a series of little daily victories."* It will not be in one big bang, but in daily little pops that have the power to change you and all that is around you. You are not who you were yesterday, you have learned and grown so much.

"In the future there is laid up for me the crown of righteousness, which the Lord, the righteous Judge, will award to me on that day; and not only to me, but also to all who have loved His appearing." — 2 Timothy 4:8

❖ ❖ ❖

Daily Thoughts: #72

THE MOST IMPORTANT

"Always bear in mind that your own resolution to succeed is more important than any other one thing."
— Abraham Lincoln

Have you ever wanted something so bad that you cannot stop thinking about it? Your desire almost consumes you and directs your every action and decision. **Success-Minded People** know that it is the strong desire, the deep determination for its fulfillment that beings dreams into reality. You are willing to do the work, pay the price for the dream. You will not let it go. As former U.S. Secretary of State, Colin Powell said, *"A dream doesn't become reality through magic; it takes sweat, determination and hard work."*

We live in a culture that too often tells people that to fulfill your dreams is easy. There are easy ways to *"get rich in your spare time"*, you can have — be — look, any way you want because (and this drives me crazy) you *"deserve"* it. **Success-Minded People** know that is not true. The fulfillment of your dreams, the achievement of your life's purpose is hard. It will take lots of hard work and determination. As the 17th century clergyman, Thomas Fuller said, *"An invincible determination can accomplish almost anything and in this lies the great distinction between great men and little men."*

Success-Minded People must understand that their level of determination will set their level of success. If you have set in your heart that you will, no question or excuses, achieve your dreams, then nothing will stop you. Author and speaker Les Brown said, *"If you set goals and go after them with all the determination you can muster, your gifts will take you places that will amaze you."* **Success-Minded People** know that they possess more power than they can see. Once they set their heart and mind on the goal, that power kicks in and things happen that would not have happened before.

Have you determined to achieve your goals? Have you set it in your heart of hearts that you will not settle for anything less than success? The great Og Mandino said, *"Failure will never overtake me if my determination to succeed is strong enough."* That determination moves you past obstacles, past objections of others, past negativity and fear, all the way to achievement. The difference between **Success-Minded People** and others is that they know, not wish – not hope – but know, they will achieve the dreams they are determined to fulfill. They will gladly work hard, take the time, energy and expense to do what they must to achieve. Never a question, success belongs to them.

"Do you see a man skilled in his work? He will stand before kings; he will not stand before obscure men."
— Proverbs 22:29

❖ ❖ ❖

Daily Thoughts: #73

MAKE GOOD CHOICES

"Every choice you make has an end result." – Zig Ziglar

There is no greater power in the entire world than the power of choice. We make choices all the time and therefore have power in our life. Even in our spiritual walk, God never, never takes away our power to choose. If we follow Him or not is up to us; He never forces us to obey His word. You cannot escape it or push it off to someone else. Choice is a reality of life and you must and will make them. As William James noted, *"When you have to make a choice and don't make it, that is in itself a choice."*

Success-Minded People know that their life will be a reflection of the choices they make. Bad choices will bring bad results; good choices, good results. This is why we need to develop wisdom in our life. Daily reading of God's Word, the Bible, along with a teachable heart that is always learning and growing will help you in making good choices. Another important key will be your attitude. People who have a negative attitude and outlook tend to make bad choices. They focus too much on themselves and what will feel good for the moment. Negative people do not look out and see the consequence of their choices; only the immediate effects they can get.

Success-Minded People on the other hand look at choices with a positive attitude. They are more outwardly focused and think about the long term. What will the choice they make mean to others and what results will it bring in the long run? These are the questions that lead to wise choices.

The fact that you need to be positive or negative in your attitude is a choice in itself. You have the power to change if you need to. Pastor and author Charles Swindoll said, *"The remarkable thing is, we have a choice everyday regarding the attitude we will embrace for that day."* The choice is yours to make and no one else's.

Author Stephen Covey said, *"There are three constants in life...change, choice and principles."* **Success-Minded People** know that the more right choices they make, the better they get at it. Will they fail at times and make a wrong choice? Of course they will, no one is perfect. But they learn from the bad choices and that too brings wisdom. To make a wrong choice once is a learning experience. To make wrong choices repeatedly is foolishness. You choose which will mark your life.

> *"If it is disagreeable in your sight to serve the Lord, choose for yourselves today whom you will serve."*
>
> – Joshua 24:15

❖ ❖ ❖

Daily Thoughts: #74

WHAT DO YOU WANT TO BE?

"First say to yourself what you would be; and then do what you have to do." — Epictetus

Not long ago I attended a men's Bible study and the topic of the evening was the parable of the Samaritan. As we discussed what this story meant to each of us, we all came to a common conclusion. The parable teaches us the importance of doing the right thing. It does not matter who you are or what you believe, God has given all living things a standard to live by and part of that is to take care of each other.

This takes my thoughts to the Boy Scout slogan, *"Do a good turn daily."* Why is that important to teach boys? Does this apply to adults as well? The principles of **Success-Minded People** that I have drawn up are based on the Boy Scout Law. I believe these principles are vital for all of us to achieve for a successful life. Doing a good turn is nothing more than doing what is right. Businessman and author W. Clement Stone said, *"Have courage to say no. Have the courage to face the truth. Do the right thing because it is right. These are the magic keys to living your life with integrity."*

Success-Minded People understand that to do the right thing is not a decision we make depending on the circumstances. It is a decision we make about life. Doing the right thing is something we do all the time and do by conscious choice. It is called integrity, and it is a characteristic of **Success-Minded People**. It is not a rule or demand on us, it is just who we are, people of integrity. French philosopher, Albert Camus said, *"Integrity has no need for rules."* People of integrity will do the right thing – every time.

As a **Success-Minded Person** remember that you will be faced with the decision to do the right thing at every turn. A person who needs help, a door to open, a wrong to be made right. There are decisions to do right all around us. Pastor David Jeremiah said, *"Integrity is keeping a commitment even after circumstances have changed."* Your commitment as a **Success-Minded Person** is to always do the right thing. It is a commitment you must stand by.

R. Buckminster Fuller said, *"Integrity is the essence of everything successful."* That is such a true statement. Your standing as a person of integrity will determine your level of success in life. A lack of integrity will never bring true success. Doing the right thing is not just something we do, it is everything we do.

"Then you will discern righteousness and justice and equity and every good course."   – Proverbs 2:9

❖ ❖ ❖

Daily Thoughts: #75

WHAT YOU COULD HAVE BEEN

"It is never too late to be what you might have been."
                                           – George Eliot

American poet, John Greenleaf Whittier in his poem Maud Muller (1856) made this insightful statement: *"For all sad words of tongue or pen, the saddest of these: 'It might have been!'"* How many people have you heard use the phrases, *"If only," "I wish I would have," "It could have been different"*? These are terms that could bring tears to your eyes. They sound so hopeless and regretful.

The good news is that you do not have to accept these statements for your life. **Success-Minded People** have all had experiences that we wish we would have done differently. We have failed to take advantage of opportunities that could have moved us forward or allowed the urgent things in life to distract us from the important. No you cannot go back and do them over, but you can change and go on from here.

There are reasons that you missed an opportunity or neglected to do what you needed to in order move forward. The answer is to change that old behavior and go on from where you are. It is never too late for change. Andy Andrews, author of <u>The Traveler's Gift</u> and other books said, *"Most people think it takes a long time to change.*

It doesn't. Change is immediate! Instantaneous! It may take a long time to decide to change...but change happens in a heartbeat." I have found that to be true in my own life. When I wanted to change, and made the decision to change, change happened right away.

Success-Minded People are not to live in regret. We have all missed the boat at some point in life, but there is always another going out. If you have a dream and know your purpose in life, it is never too late to do something about it. God has given you dreams that He has always intended for you to achieve. If He could give a child to Abraham and Sarah in their old age, He can fulfill your dreams too. All you have to do is go after them. It still takes change and commitment along with hard work, but you can do it.

The key to all success (**Success-Minded People** know this) is action. Author Dick Biggs put it this way, *"The greatest gap in life is the one between knowing and doing."* It is time for action my friend. The time has come to be who you were created to be. **Success-Minded People** should never need to utter the words, *"It might have been."*

"Whatever you do, do your work heartily, as for the Lord rather than for men." – Colossians 3:23

❖ ❖ ❖

Daily Thoughts: #76

ACTING THE PART

"Believe and act as if it were impossible to fail."
– Charles F. Kettering

I f you knew you could not fail at achieving your dream and life purpose, how would you act? Now think about this. There is a way we act, move, breath and think when we are fully confident of success. How would that look for you? Success is not just an action; it is a state of mind, a belief system that allows us to move forward with courage and determination. In short, success takes faith.

Scripture tells us in Hebrews 11 that *"Faith is the assurance of things hoped for, the convictions of things not seen."* It then goes on to list the achievements of those who believed in their task and had the faith to achieve. It is not based on what they saw or had evidence of, but what they believed God could and would do. Seventeenth Century Christian philosopher Blaise Pascal said, *"Faith is a sounder guide than reason. Reason can go only so far, but faith has no limits."*

So again I ask you: How would you act and think if you knew you could not fail? **Success-Minded People** know that the key to their success is in this question. That is because you will begin to achieve when you act and think like an achiever. **Success-Minded People** are not successful after they have achieved their dream. They have been successful all along. It is because they knew they were successful that they could achieve.

The greatest enemy of faith is fear. Fear of failure or that the task is too big, or that things will go wrong, or that you will make a fool of yourself. There is always an element of fear in stepping out, but you must control it and not allow it to control you. Author Katherine Paterson said, *"To fear is one thing. To let fear grab you by the tail and swing you around is another."* Never allow fear to have the upper hand. Faith can and does overcome fear.

Take some time alone and think about who you need to be to succeed. How would you walk, talk, breath, think and work. Write it down in as much detail as possible. Read this everyday and start to act on it. It is not faking it. This is who you are. If you believe God has given you a dream, that He has called you to fulfill a purpose in life, then it is so. All you are doing is acting like the **Success-Minded Person** you really are.

Faith is the most powerful weapon we have against fear and negativity. Read through Hebrews 11 and see how people, just like you and me, believed God and changed the world.

"In whom we have boldness and confident access through faith in Him."   – Ephesians 3:12

❖ ❖ ❖

Daily Thoughts: #77

MORPHING

"I know for sure that what we dwell on is who we become."
– Oprah Winfrey

Success-Minded People know that what they focus on is what will become, whether that is success and achievement, or fear and failure. But I want to come at this from a bit of a different angle. How does this apply to us as Christians? American clergyman Henry Ward Beecher said, *"A Christian is nothing but a sinful man who has put himself to school for Christ for the honest purpose of becoming better."* As Christians, we are called to be different, changed from what we were and an example to the world.

From what I have seen in the lives of my fellow believers, there are two different beliefs among Christians. One is that they are dreadful sinners, and the other that Christ is a wonderful savior. Both are true, but both can cause different results. For the one who focuses on their sin and unworthiness, they become defeated and depressed. They know that there is nothing they can do to deserve the forgiveness and redemption that Christ offers. They are forever caught in this downward spin, missing out on the joy and freedom that is also offered in Christ.

For the one who I will call the **Success-Minded Christian**, they understand that it is not about what they deserve. Jesus Christ came to save the lost, and that is us. He freely gives forgiveness and eternal life because there is no way we could earn it. We live for Him not to win His favor, but because of His favor. Pastor and Professor Sinclair B. Ferguson said, *"There is nothing more important to learn about Christian growth than this: Growing in grace means becoming like Christ."*

Success-Minded Christians focus their thought on who Christ is and what that means to us as sinners. As with anything is the success process, it is not easy to grow in Christ. The Purpose Driven Life author Rick Warren said, *"Becoming like Christ is a long, slow process of growth."* It is everyday and in everything we do. We are to be like Christ in thought word and deed. I don't know about you, but for me that is a tall order, one I daily struggle with, but gladly follow.

The better you know Jesus the more you will be like Him. Pastor Harry Emerson Fosdick said, *"The steady discipline of intimate friendship with Jesus results in men becoming like Him."* Get to know Him better than anyone else in your life. Read His Word, the Bible, pray and live for Him alone. He loves you and wants you more than you want Him.

"And do not be conformed to this world, but be transformed by the renewing of your mind, so that you may prove what the will of God is..." – Romans 12:2

❖ ❖ ❖

Daily Thoughts: #78

BUYING THE TICKET

"You are today where your thoughts have brought you; you will be tomorrow where your thoughts take you."
— James Allen

Thoughts are very powerful things. They are able to create things which before have not been, change the course of human events and bring down mighty armies. How can that be? Well, everything that is was once a thought in someone's mind. Even the creation itself was in the thoughts of God. That is why this principle works. We, all mankind, were created in His image, which means many of the characteristics of God are in us, the ability to create, think, love and be compassionate. I am not saying we are little gods; that is not true, I am saying we have some of our Father's characteristics.

Author James Allen wrote a landmark book back in 1903 titled <u>As a Man Thinketh</u>, which is still in publication today. In that book he makes a clear and simple statement, *"Good thoughts bear good fruit, bad thoughts create bad fruit."* Put another way, what you put into your mind will give you equal results. A simple truth yet so often ignored. Too many people spend their time watching violence and filth and wonder why they cannot succeed in life. They spend their day with thoughts on hate and anger and wonder why they have problems with health and attitude.

Former British Prime Minister, Benjamin Disraeli said, *"Nurture your mind with great thoughts. To believe in the heroic makes heroes."* When we fill our thought with what is good, right, just, wholesome and honorable, we become that type of person. When our thoughts are on success and achievement we tend to be successful and achieving people. **Success-Minded People** know that their thoughts today will show up in their success tomorrow.

If you feel stuck and not moving in the direction you wish to go, look at your thoughts. Are they positive and excited or negative and fearful? Start to focus them on what you are trying to achieve. Inventor Alexander Graham Bell said, *"Concentrate all your thoughts upon the task at hand. The sun's rays do not burn until brought into focus."*

Scripture tells us that as a man thinks in his heart, so is he. What is in your heart? **Success-Minded People** are just that – *success-minded.* **Success-Minded People** know that God is their Father, and they are a chip off the old block. They want and work to be like Him. There is nothing more positive in this life than to be a child of the Living God and to walk in the path He has set for you. We should all long to be like our Heavenly Father.

"For whatever is born of God overcomes the world; and this is the victory that has overcome the world – our faith."
– 1 John 5:4

❖ ❖ ❖

Daily Thoughts: #79

POWER THINKING

"Man's greatness lies in his power of thought."
— Blaise Pascal

Success-Minded People cultivate their imagination like a farmer does his garden. He knows how to care for the plants that will be growing there. He understands the importance of nourishing the soil in which they will be planted. He knows what plants grow best near others, and how big he expects them to grow. He waters and tills the soil regularly. Most important he keeps the weeds out and does not allow pests to destroy his plants. In the end, a rich and healthy harvest is his reward.

This also applies to the **Success-Minded Person** who cares for his thoughts and keeps the weeds of negativity and fear out. In the end he will be rewarded with success. It is all a matter of focus. Success teacher Brian Tracy said, *"The key to success is to focus our conscious mind on the things we desire, not things we fear."* I will dare to say that most of the work that goes into success is in the mind. Again, as with the farmer, the **Success-Minded Person** focuses on the details of the garden, the plant grows naturally by itself.

Success-Minded People understand that the only limit to their success lies in them. Likewise, the power to succeed also lies in them. Founder of Success Magazine, Orison Sweet Marden said, *"Our thoughts and imagination are the only real limits to our possibilities."* If you are willing to apply these principles of success and to keep a positive mind set and attitude, you can do great things. Not perhaps you can – you *can* do them.

One way that you can nourish the soil of your thoughts is to keep learning. Read all you can, go to seminars and workshops and take classes. Most important, be around positive and successful people. Always surround yourself with people who are better than you. People who think better thoughts. People who do what you do, only better than you do. These people will bring you up and build you up. If all you have are friends who are on your level or below, you have nowhere to go. Remember what Ralph Waldo Emerson said, "*Our best thoughts come from others.*"

You have the choice to make the garden of your mind blossom into an abundant harvest or just become a bed of weeds. If you do not care for the garden daily, the weeds will grow all on their own. You must tend to your thoughts daily to be rewarded with that good harvest.

"When my anxious thoughts multiply within me, Your consolations delight my soul."   – Psalm 94:19

❖ ❖ ❖

Daily Thoughts: #80

GOT NERVE?

"Anything's possible if you've got enough nerve."
— J.K. Rowling

M any like the idea of being a **Success-Minded Person**. The whole concept of being successful is very appealing to people. But when you add to it things like hard work and the character of a **Success-Minded Person** being honorable, faithful, a servant, a friend, mannerly, caring, responsible, positive, frugal, courageous, healthy and spiritually committed, people tend to change their tune. *"That is just too much work,"* they say. The truth is it takes a great deal of courage to be a **Success-Minded Person.**

When I talk with groups about personal achievement and the success principles, I always make sure they understand that true success is possible, but not easy. Former President Ronald Reagan said, *"There are no easy answers' but there are simple answers. We must have the courage to do what we know is morally right."* If you are not willing to do what is right or brave enough to stand for right in a world that tends to glorify wrong, then you will never enjoy true success.

Success-Minded People know that to live by the fundamental principles of success you will have to take a stand for what is right. Success is not made up of wealth and titles or positions; it is a way of life. **Success-Minded People** live the principles every day. It is not just a technique that they try to do in order to get what they want. It is how they think and behave. True success is reflected in how we view life and treat other people.

Those people who want the material rewards of success but not the lifestyle do not have the courage to make it. They will have their excuses that it's too hard or that it's old fashioned and no longer needed. As French philosopher Albert Camus said, *"Those who lack courage will always find a philosophy to justify it."* These are the excuse-makers in life. They are the ones who cry for what is "fair," and they want their share of the pie. In the end, they will be left behind and live off the scraps of those who had the courage to go on.

As a **Success-Minded Person** you will do what is right and stand for right. You may have a set back or two, but you will go on. As Sir Winston Churchill said, *"Success is not final, failure is not fatal: it is the courage to continue that counts."* There is a power, a confidence that comes over you when you know that you stand for what is right, when you live a successful life. No one can take that away from you.

> *"In the fear of the Lord there is strong confidence, and His children will have refuge."*   – Proverbs 14:26

❖ ❖ ❖

Daily Thoughts: #81

YOUR FIRST STEPS

"Take the first step in faith. You don't have to see the whole staircase. Just take the first step."
– Martin Luther King, Jr.

A common question I am asked is, *"How do I get started?"* I know they are waiting for a five-point plan to get them on their way. I am afraid that my answer is a simple one: Get started. To start you have to do something – anything. I remember John Maxwell once said that people often ask him, *"How do I become a writer?"* His answer: You write. He said he was amazed at how many people who want to become writers never write a word. Without acting in the direction of your goal, you will never achieve a thing.

There are many reasons for people not starting, but I believe the main one is they just have not decided what they want to do or whether they want to pay the price for it. Author of the bestselling book, Think and Grow Rich, Napoleon Hill said, *"The way to develop decisiveness is to start right where you are, with the very next question you face."* First decide what you want to do, and then take the first step.

Success-Minded People understand that it is not what you know that will begin the process of success, it is what you do. Start with what you have and where you are. It does not have to be something big and grand; success builds as it goes. Here is a method that works for many: Write down your goal. To achieve that, what do you have to do?

If starting at the end and working backwards is easier, do that. List all the steps that you have to do to achieve the goal. Now take the list, go to number one, and do it.

Success-Minded People must have faith to move forward. They need faith in themselves, faith in God and faith in the dream. You do not have to have proof that you are doing the right thing at the right time. You need to trust your gut and move. Believe that God will direct you. Former Chaplin of Harvard University, D. Elton Trueblood said, *"Faith is not belief without proof, but trust without reservation."*

The first step is always just to take action. God will direct and guide you, but you must be moving first. There is an old saying: *"You can only steer a moving train."* Without some kind of action you will just stand still. Make the action connected to the goal you are trying to achieve. If you want to be a writer, write, a painter, paint, a salesperson, sell. Whatever your goal, get moving on the first step and the next step will be there when you need it.

"The mind of man plans his way, but the Lord directs his steps."   – Proverbs 16:9

❖ ❖ ❖

Daily Thoughts: #82

JOY! JOY! JOY!

"What you are here to do is what will give you the greatest amount of joy when you are doing it." – Jack Canfield

We talk so much about the hard work and commitment that has to go into a successful effort. This principle is so important to understand. Too many have started their journey to success only to give up because they were not prepared to pay the price. But there is another side to the journey that is of equal importance. That is the fact that pursuing your dream can be the best fun of your life.

Success-Minded People love what they do. It is their dream and they are enjoying every moment of the adventure. Businessman Warren Buffett said, *"We enjoy the process far more than the proceeds."* **Success-Minded People** know that the best jobs are the ones you love so much that you would do them for free. **Success-Minded People** look forward to each day they can grow and move closer to the goal. There is an excitement that they do not get from anything else.

You can tell when you are working with someone who loves what they do. They are positive, productive and have a good outlook. These are people who do their job well and take the time to get things right. There is a pride that goes into their work. As poet Samuel Butler said, *"People are always good company when they are doing what they really enjoy."*

Success-Minded People know that when they are doing what they love they have more energy, more joy in life and are able to rest better. Fifteenth century Monk Thomas a Kempis said, *"The reflections on a day well spent furnish us with joys more pleasing than ten thousand triumphs."* There are few things that are as satisfying as to look back over your day and know you did your best and your best was excellent.

Yes, it is hard work to go after your dream. It takes effort, learning and continual growth. It may take you years to achieve your goals, but they can be the best years of your life. Author and speaker, Zig Ziglar says, *"You do not pay the price of success; you enjoy the price of success."* The pursuit of your dream, your main purpose in life is an adventure that consumes your life. You may try to walk away at times, but you will always come back to it. The dream calls to you all day, all night. You know that you will never be happy until you have started the great adventure that will change it all. Go for it and have fun!

"He makes us pay for exactly what we've done – no more, no less. Our chickens always come home to roost."

– Job 34:11

❖ ❖ ❖

Daily Thoughts: #83

FIND A WAY

"If you really want to do something, you'll find a way; if you don't you'll find an excuse." — Unknown

Success-Minded People know that there is no giving up when pursuing your dream. Many people do, but that is a choice, not an outcome. When faced with a mountain, **Success-Minded People** will go over it, through it, or around it, but however it happens they will be on the other side. That is called determination. Author Denis Waitley said, *"Determination gives you the resolve to keep going in spite of the roadblocks that lay before you."*

There are two kinds of people on the road to success. One is the person who has an excuse for not achieving their dream. They will blame the economy, their parents, their employer, their spouse, society or even God for their falling short. George Washington Carver rightly said, *"Ninety-nine percent of the failures come from people who have the habit of making excuses."* As soon as I hear an excuse, I know this person will never make it unless they are willing to change and become responsible for their life.

The other person is the **Success-Minded Person**, who, may not have made it yet but is still moving forward. They offer no excuses because no excuse is needed. They know that success is a process and they are just working through the process. I think Olympic Wrestling Gold Medalist, Dan Gable said it best: *"Gold medals aren't really made of gold.*

They're made of sweat, determination and a hard-to-find alloy called guts." **Success-Minded People** have guts!

Success-Minded People need to understand that we are not allowed to know the details of tomorrow. We know that there will be trials and difficulties along the way, but there is no room for excuses on the road to success. Success is not dependent on how hard a task will be; it is always the fact that you will not stop or go back. Another Olympic Gold Medalist, Charles Simmons said, *"Never go backward. Attempt, and do it with all your might. Determination is power."* When you are out for the prize, there is no holding back.

Success-Minded People never ask themselves the question, "What if I don't make it." They do not have "back-up" jobs or an escape plan if things go wrong. If you prepare for failure, you will fail. If you have an out, I can promise you that the time will come where you will take it. **Success-Minded People** burn their boats and blow up their bridges. Failure is not an option. That means only one thing, they must succeed. And succeed they will.

"A little sleep, a little slumber, a little folding of the hands to rest. Your poverty will come in like a vagabond and your need like an armed man." — Proverbs 6:10–11

❖ ❖ ❖

Daily Thoughts: #84

WHAT WAS I THINKING?

"The biggest mistake people make in life is not trying to make a living at doing what they most enjoy."

— Malcolm S. Forbes

When I am coaching a person about their career I often ask the question, *"What do you want to do?"* They most often start giving me a list of what they can do. I again ask the question, *"What do you WANT to do?"* Then I hear about what they think God wants them to do. Still seeking an answer, I ask, *"But what do YOU want to do."* At this point I usually get a puzzled look and a simple, *"I don't know."*

You see, you do not have to settle for what you have done, what you are trained to do or what someone else tells you that you should do. I believe that in every **Success-Minded Person** is the desire to do something. Call it your dream, purpose or drive, but you know what it is. When you have time to dream, you dream about it. When faced with making life decisions, you think about it. You may think it is impossible, but you really want it. Thomas Carlyle said, *"Every noble work is at first impossible."*

Then there is the question, *"What is God's will?"* Do you think that God is going to design you for a purpose and make you do something you hate? He will place in you the desire to do His will. Also, do not make the mistake in thinking that God's will for us is only spiritual or in ministry. God puts His people in all walks of life. The Christian businessperson can be in the center of God's will as much as the Pastor.

President Theodore Roosevelt said, *"Far and away the best prize that life offers is the chance to work hard at work worth doing."* I do not believe anyone should be working at a job they hate. This is America, and we have choices. You can find the job you love or make it. It is up to you. No excuses as to how hard it is, you are too old, too young, broke or under educated. If you are a **Success-Minded Person**, you will find away.

So let me ask you, *"What do you want to do?"* What is the job you would love to have? As a **Success-Minded Person** you should be able to answer that question. If not, think about it. It is never meant to be a mystery. Doing the job you love will change your life. You will become more productive and driven to succeed. Pastor Sam Storms says, *"Enjoyment empowers effort. Doing is the fruit of delight. Performance is energized by pleasure."*

"For the ways of a man are before the eyes of the Lord, and He watches all his paths." – Proverbs 5:21

❖ ❖ ❖

Daily Thoughts: #85

WORK WITH WHAT YOU HAVE

"Use what talents you possess; the woods would be very silent if no birds sang except those that sang best."
— Henry Van Dyke

How many times have you wanted to use a gift or talent you have but decided to wait till you were *"good enough"*? I think most of us have at one time or other. The problem is that we seldom do get better. Why? Because we are not using our talent. Talents get better the more we use them. Sure, at first you may be a bit rough, but the more you practice and the more you use your talents, the better you get. As that great American Statesman, Benjamin Franklin said, *"Hide not your talents. They for use were made. What's a sundial in the shade?"*

When I am talking about talents, I do not mean just those that would be considered in the arts world. Singing, dancing, painting and so on are all great, and do apply here, but there are more. Some have talents in business or ministry or in organizational skills. We all have something to give. Gymnast, Mary Lou Retton said, *"As simple as it sounds, we all must try to be the best person we can: by making the best choices, by making the most of the talents we've been given."* Remember, the better you are, the better we all are.

What are you really good at? What do you think is a true talent that you have? You don't have to be the best at it yet, that takes time. Talents are like muscles; the more you work them, the stronger they get. Educator, John W. Gardner said, *"True happiness involves the full use of one's power and talents."* Using your talents will make you stronger, happier and build that sense of confidence you need to succeed.

Success-Minded People know that their talents are not giving just so they can feel better about themselves. Talents are given so we can serve others and make the world we live in better as a whole. Our talents are gifts from the Lord for us to give away, not to hide and peek at when we are alone. You have to use them daily to build their full effect. If you don't, like muscles they will atrophy and die away. The great Industrialist, Andrew Carnegie said, *"People who are unable to motivate themselves must be content with mediocrity, no matter how impressive their other talents."* You were not created for mediocrity. You are a **Success-Minded Person** and your talents are there to bless others and to change your world.

Don't wait for the *"right time"* to develop your natural talents. Now is the right time. Today is your day to succeed. You have all you need; you just have to use it.

"But encourage one another day after day, as long as it is still called 'Today', so that none of you will be hardened by the deceitfulness of sin." — Hebrews 5:13

❖ ❖ ❖

Daily Thoughts: #86

MAKING ADJUSTMENTS

"Don't let what you can't do stop you from doing what you can do."   – John Wooden

Success-Minded People understand the difference between strengths and weaknesses. We live in a culture that tells us that we should find our weaknesses and make them our strengths. I am sorry, but that cannot be done. Put simply, strengths make you strong and weaknesses make you weak. It is much better to find your strengths and build on them. That will take you from being good to being excellent. Focusing on weaknesses will only take you from bad to not-so-good. Who wants that?

As a **Success-Minded Person** you need to identify your strengths and abilities. What are you good at? Then you need to use those strengths as much as you can. The same principle applies for your weaknesses. What are you not good at or do not like to do? Then you have to do them less. Strengths expert and bestselling author Marcus Buckingham simply says *"Discover what you don't like doing, and stop doing it."* I know that sounds silly, but it works.

Many years ago I read Buckingham's book, <u>The One Thing</u>. In it he talks about ways to get away from your weaknesses. One suggestion was to stop doing something you were not good at, and see if anyone noticed. I did that and much to my surprise, no one noticed. Many of us do things just because we think we are supposed to or because an old job description says we should. But instead of allowing yourself to be rated on the things you do not do well, draw attention to the things you are great at.

Success-Minded People need to know where to put their energies and why. Know what you are not good at and either stop doing it or get someone else to do it. You are in the same boat as your fellow workers; they too have things they do not like doing. Find someone who likes what you do not like and does not like what you are good at and trade. It's a simple solution that makes everyone's job better.

Working in your strengths is the ability to know yourself and make adjustments that improve your performance. Tony Robbins said, *"Stay committed to your decisions, but stay flexible in your approach."* On the road to success you will always come across things that you are not good at as well as those you are. Be flexible and make changes where you need to. This does not change your destination, but it will make the journey so much nicer.

"Have I not commanded you? Be strong and courageous! Do not tremble or be dismayed, for the Lord your God is with you wherever you go."   – Joshua 1:9

❋ ❋ ❋

Daily Thoughts: #87

ACHIEVE! ACHIEVE!

"Think of yourself as on the threshold of unparalleled success. A whole clear, glorious life lies before you. Achieve! Achieve!" — Andrew Carnegie

Author Wilfred A. Peterson said, *"Big thinking precedes great achievement."* One thing all **Success-Minded People** are is big thinkers. The dreams and desires of **Success-Minded People** go far beyond their abilities. They know that the impossible is achievable for those who think big. **Success-Minded People** agree with the words of the great medical missionary, David Livingstone: *"I determined never to stop until I have come to the end and achieved my purpose."*

Success-Minded People also know that just because they believe they can achieve, it will not happen without action. They must do the work necessary to accomplish their dreams. Successful businessman and philanthropist, Bo Bennett stated, *"A dream becomes a goal when action is taken toward its achievement."* So what is needed to make this transition from dream to goal? I believe there are three key elements that must be present for any dream to be achieved.

First, you must know exactly what you want. Be clear and detailed in what it is you are trying to achieve. Businessman and author W. Clement Stone said, *"Definiteness of purpose is the starting point of all achievement."* Know what it is you are after.

Second, you must be prepared for what you are going to achieve. Robert H. Schuller, Pastor of the Crystal Cathedral, said *"Spectacular achievement is always preceded by unspectacular preparation."* Learn what you need to know, be ready for what must be done. If you are not prepared, you will not be able to act when the time comes.

Third, is prayer. Never be so foolish as to think you can achieve anything without the help of God. **Success-Minded People** know this: Without God they are nothing, but with God they can do anything He asks. Evangelist E.M. Bounds said, *"The story of great Christian achievement is the history of answered prayer."* Through prayer we get direction, wisdom in making choices and strength to face the battles ahead.

As a **Success-Minded Person** you have all you need to achieve great things. The time has come to start taking the actions that will bring the things you desire to your door. You and God make a winning team. Now: Achieve! Achieve!

"I love those who love Me; and those who diligently seek Me will find Me. Riches and honor are with Me, enduring wealth and righteousness."   – Proverbs 8:17-18

❖ ❖ ❖

Daily Thoughts: #88

WHAT DO YOU EXPECT?

"We tend to live up to our expectations."
— Earl Nightingale

I knew a man who worked for years at the principles of success. He read all the books, listened to the CDs and went to many seminars. He appeared to all as having been the model of a **Success-Minded Person** with one important exception. He did not succeed at a single thing he tried. I asked him one day, why is it that you do all the right things but do not get the right results? His answer said it all. *"I never expected to succeed,"* he said, *"nothing ever works out for me."* My friend expected failure and that was just what he got.

Author and speaker, Brian Tracy rightly said, *"We will always tend to fulfill our own expectations of ourselves."* Understanding the principles of success is important, but you will never succeed if you do not expect to. In fact, I would dare say that you can succeed by expectation without knowing the principles of success, faster than you can by knowing all the right stuff and expecting to fail. Inventor Charles Kettering said, *"High achievement always takes place in the framework of high expectation."*

Success-Minded People know that by following the principles of success, and trusting in God's direction, they will achieve their dreams and purposes. They win because they expect to win. **Success-Minded People** know that they can never expect too much. Pastor and teacher, A.B. Simpson said, *"Our God has boundless resources. The only limit is in us. Our asking, our thinking, our praying are too small. Our expectations are too limited."*

As you pursue your dream, what are you expecting to happen? Do you expect to achieve, or do you expect to fail? Do you expect to succeed quickly or to come in a distant second? **Success-Minded People** know that even when they do expect to succeed, their expectation is most likely too small. They understand that we serve a great God, not an adequate God. He can and does do more than we can expect or think. The great Charles Spurgeon said, *"God has great things in store for His people; they ought to have large expectations."*

You may not have to have it all together or be on a successful track to expect great things. But you can do that from where you are this minute. Former Governor and Presidential candidate, Mike Huckabee said, *"It's when ordinary people rise above their expectations and seize the opportunity, that milestones truly are reached."* Keep your expectations high and boldly move forward in your pursuit of your dreams. You can do great things if you believe you can.

> *"Now to Him who is able to do far more abundantly beyond all that we ask or think, according to the power that works within us."* – Ephesians 3:20

❖ ❖ ❖

Daily Thoughts: #89

WINNING THE GAME

"It's the job that's never started that takes the longest to finish."   – J.R.R. Tolkien

Success-Minded People know that it is important to start well, to be prepared, have a plan and begin the journey. They also know that it is more important to finish well. As Pastor and teacher, Woodrow Kroll said, *"Finishing well brings more glory to God than beginning well."* We may still be a ways from the finish line, but we can prepare now to finish well.

For the **Success-Minded Person**, the journey is the most fun. Yes we want to achieve our dreams and goals in life. Please notice that I said dreams and goals – plural. You will not have just one dream or goal; you should have many. God did not create you to be a one-hit-wonder. You were made to achieve and keep on achieving all your life.

The first step is to have that vision and not give up till you have achieved it. Novelist, Thomas Hardy said, *"Good business leaders create a vision, articulate the vision, passionately own the vision, and relentlessly drive it to completion."* Once that vision is achieved, it is on to the next. Actually, your vision should be a series of goals and steps. You do not achieve and rest, you move right to the next.

"There is no short cut to achievement." said George Washington Carver, *"Life requires thorough preparation – veneer isn't worth anything."* **Success-Minded People** know this

journey will take them the rest of their life to complete. There will be rewards and satisfaction along the way, but there will always be a new horizon for which to reach. At the end, there is the ultimate goal of life, to reach the distant shore and hear the words, *"Well done, My good and faithful servant."*

I know that you have put a lot of work into your dreams so far. Some have seen benefits already; some are still plugging along. I can promise you that it is only a start. The journey is sweeter each day. Evangelist, Ravi Zacharias said, *"Beginning well is a momentary thing; finishing well is a lifelong thing."* And if I may add, the rewards are eternal.

Stay faithful to the path God has put you on. If you still have not begun your journey to success, now is the time. Step out and make today your time to begin well. If you are a **Success-Minded Person** who has been on this road a long time, remember that it is the journey, not the destination that is all the fun. Enjoy yourself as you achieve greatness in yourself and glory for God.

"Prepare your work outside, and make it ready for yourself in the field; afterwards then build your house."
– Proverbs 24:27

❖ ❖ ❖

Daily Thoughts: #90

THE NOT-SO-HIDDEN POWER

"If we wish to free ourselves from enslavement, we must choose freedom and the responsibility this entails."

– Leo Buscaglia

Success-Minded People have a great responsibility in life. Since we are learning the ways of a successful life and what it means to stand for what is good and right, we must share that information with the world we live in. Not our opinion on things but the principles of the **Success-Minded Person**. This is what we will one day answer for: how we added value to our world. As Mark Driscoll, Pastor of Mars Hill Church in Seattle said, *"In the end, our opinion does not really matter. We will not die and stand before a mirror to give account."*

This is why **Success-Minded People** need to be involved in their communities and the world that God has placed them in. They should be in business, politics, religious work, community service and education. I feel C.S. Lewis put it best when he said, *"What we want is not more books about Christianity, but more books by Christians on other subjects."* Remember that we are to be a light to the world.

Too often people, even **Success-Minded People**, think that Christians are only to deal with spiritual things and leave the *"secular world"* alone. That is not the command we have from the Lord. We are to show the world what it means to be a believer in Jesus Christ by the life we lead. Christians should be the most upright, honest, caring and hard working people in the community. Others should know us because we live the principles we talk about, not because we insist that others live by them.

Christianity is not a religion, but a life style. It is who we are, not just what we believe. Do not allow the world to define you or restrict you. Just be who you are and be the example of how believers live. Like Paul told young Timothy, we are to show in *"speech, conduct, love, faith and purity"* an example of those that believe. We are the only Bible most people will read. We are what most will come to know as a **Success-Minded Person**. If it isn't real for us, if it doesn't work for us, they will never accept it.

Our purpose here is to be the example. We are to be salt and light in a dark and dying world. It is a big responsibility but it comes with success. If one of us fails, we all fail. Together we can see things change for the better. God made us for this moment.

"The Lord has made everything for its own purpose."
– Proverbs 16:4

❖ ❖ ❖

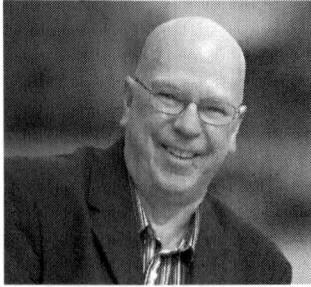

John Patrick Hickey, CPVA, CPBA, CLC, has been coaching leaders and individuals and building teams for three decades. He has a personal passion to help **Success-Minded People** identify their giftings, set goals and achieve their dreams, while becoming the best they can be. John is a gifted team coach and knows how to help leaders build teams that are enriching for all its members and that accomplish their objectives.

John's organization, The Growth Center LLC, provides three key services to help you, your company, your church, organization, school and family move from good to great: coaching and mentoring; assessment and testing, and church and corporate team building. John is also available to speak at your meeting or conference, delivering encouraging, inspirational messages that will move your audience towards their dreams.

To learn more about The Growth Center LLC, *visit www.growthcenter.net*. To book for your next event, write us at *leadership@growthcenter.net*.

"Where success is concerned, people are not measured in inches, or pounds, or college degrees, or family backgrounds; they are measured by the size of their thinking." – Davis Schwartz

Stay on the journey. Visit www.90dailythoughts.com for encouragement, inspiration, as well as dialogue with other Success-Minded People.

Made in the USA
Charleston, SC
27 August 2011